D1240836

Copyright © 2023 by O N A M I

All rights reserved. No part of this publication may be reproduced,
distributed, or transmitted in any form or by any means, including
photocopying, recording, or other electronic or mechanical methods,
without the prior written permission of the publisher, except in the
case of brief quotations embodied in critical reviews and certain other
noncommercial uses permitted by copyright law. For permission requests,
write to the publisher, addressed "Attention: Permissions Coordinator," at
the address below.

Onami House
Box 768
Santa Fe, NM
87321

Printed in the United States of America
Publisher's Cataloging-in-Publication data

O N A M I
Fuckless The Workbook / O N A M I

ISBN 9798394049446

The main category of the book —Self Help —Other category. 2. Another
subject category —Education. 3. More categories —And their modifiers. I.
O N A M I. II. Title. HF0000.

A0 A00 2030
299.000 00–dc22 2010989999
First Edition
1413128110/10987654321

it's your time. Nothing can stop an idea whose time has come. You can handle this. You are going to start hearing a new story about yourself very soon. A story about how you created mind-blowing success that shifted the success story for generations.

legacy shit homie.

in spite of all odds you fulfilled your destiny. HERO!

Do you even understand? Your photo is going to hang on walls for generations and generations because you tapped that ancestral magic that had lain dormant for so long.

You can do this. You were made for this.

WORK HARD
SHOW UP
EAT LIKE A GOD

Enjoy the ride baby. Plenty of room at the top.

ONAMI

fuckless

THE OBJECTIVE, STEP-BY-STEP
FORMULA TO TOTAL AUTHENTICITY

ONAMI

table of contents

ONAMI

introduction

THIS BOOK IS DEDICATED TO YOU. BECAUSE I KNOW YOU BY KNOWING MYSELF, WHICH PEOPLE ALSO CALL NARCISSISM, I'LL DEDICATE IT TO ME, WHICH WILL APPLY TO YOU, AND THEN I'LL QUICKLY EXPLAIN THE DUAL FUNCTION OF NARCISSISM BECAUSE SO MANY OF YOU ARE AFRAID OF BEING CALLED THAT.

THIS BOOK IS DEDICATED TO YOU. I SEE YOU HONEY. GOING TO SPEAK AND THEN CLOSING YOUR MOUTH. GOING TO COMMENT AND THEN TELLING YOURSELF TO SHUT UP. SAYING SOMETHING REAL AND THEN DELETING IT. SPEAKING YOUR TRUTH AND WATCHING PEOPLE'S REACTION WITH A PIT OF HUNGER IN YOUR STOMACH LIKE "AM I GOING TO BE OKAY?".

I SEE YOU PUTTING THE WHOLE WORLD BEFORE YOURSELF. I SEE YOU CARING FOR PEOPLE WHEN YOU THOUGHT IT WAS YOUR TURN. I SEE YOU CREDITING OTHER PEOPLE FOR YOUR OWN THEORIES, YOUR OWN KNOWING. I SEE YOU TRYING TO ASSEMBLE A CAREER OUT OF ALL THE MOST SUPERFICIAL LAYERS OF YOUR INTERESTS. I SEE YOU STARTING TO QUESTION IF THE THRIVING RELATIONSHIPS YOU HAVE ARE ONLY THERE BECAUSE YOU TELL THEM WHAT THEY WANT TO HEAR (ONLY ONE WAY TO FIND OUT). I SEE YOUR FEAR OF REJECTION AND YOUR DECIMATING LONELINESS WHEN YOU ARE REJECTED. I SEE YOUR "FRIENDS" DISAPPEARING WHEN YOU'RE REAL WITH THEM. I SEE IT ALL BABY. AND I'M HERE TO TELL YOU THAT THERE IS NOTHING WRONG WITH YOU, THAT THIS IS A PART OF YOUR SPIRITUAL JOURNEY THAT IS SO NECESSARY.

THERE IS NOTHING WRONG WITH YOU. IF YOU CHANGE, IF YOU'RE HONEST, THESE PEOPLE WILL REALIZE THAT THEY COULD CHANGE, AND COULD BE HONEST. THAT'S SCARY, AND YOU'RE BRAVE.

I WANT YOU TO KNOW THAT WHEN THIS WORKSHOP IS DONE, EVERY SINGLE TEAR YOU'VE EVER CRIED WILL WORK IT'S WAY INTO A PAYCHECK FOR YOU AT SOME POINT. INCLUDING AND MOST ESPECIALLY THE TEARS YOU'VE CRIED ALONE. I WANT YOU TO KNOW THAT WHEN THIS IS DONE YOU WILL BE, LIKE PEELING AN ORANGE, REVEALING YOUR JUICIEST SELF. KIND OF LIKE HOW AS A KID YOU NEED AN ADULT TO HELP YOU GET THE PEEL STARTED, BUT ONCE THEY DO YOU SEE THAT YOU CAN EASILY KEEP GOING. THAT'S WHAT THIS DOES, AND IT'S AN ENNEAGRAM SO IT'S CYCLICAL AND REUSABLE. SO KEEP GOING! AND KEEP THAT SIGN FROM VIDEO ONE UP UNTIL IT'S DONE WITH YOU.

I ALSO WANT YOU BUSINESS OWNERS TO KNOW THAT IF SHARING YOUR TRUTH IS A PART OF YOUR BRANDING (IT SHOULD BE) YOU'LL START TO SEE A BIG UPTICK IN INTEREST AND SALES (PROVIDING YOU HAVE SOMETHING FOR SALE). LET THIS BE NOT ONLY THE BEGINNING OF YOUR MISSION OF TRUTH, BUT ALSO THE BEGINNING OF A NEVER ENDING CONVERSATION YOU HAVE WITH YOURSELF ABOUT BUSINESS. STUDY BUSINESS BOOKS AND COURSES, AND PICK UP A BUSINESS BOOK FOR EVERY SPIRITUAL BOOK YOU FIND. THESE ARE THE MIRACLES YOU'VE BEEN PRAYING FOR, AS THEY WILL TEACH YOU THE VEHICLES YOU CAN SEND YOUR TRUTH OUT IN AND CAUSE A TRANSFORMATION IN THE WORLD.

IF YOU'RE VULNERABLE, SHOWING YOUR NECK TO THE VAMPIRE OF THE WORLD, YOU'RE TELLING THE WORLD "I KNOW YOU COULD HURT ME, BUT I'M NOT AFRAID" WHICH ALSO TELLS THE WORLD "I COULD HURT YOU, BUT YOU CAN TRUST ME.

I KNOW YOU BECAUSE I KNOW MYSELF. NARCISSUS LOOKED TO OTHERS FOR LOVE FOR A LONG TIME, THEN ONE DAY HE LOOKED AT HIMSELF IN THE WATER, WHICH ALWAYS MEANS "TRUTH" IN MYTHOLOGY. HE REALLY, TRULY, DEEPLY LOOKED AT HIMSELF AND HE SAW HIMSELF IN THE TOTALITY. HE SAW HIMSELF IN NOT JUST IN EVERYONE, BUT ALL OF EXISTENCE AND HE COULD NEVER LOOK AWAY.

WHEN THIS HAPPENED HE HAD NO CHOICE BUT TO TREAT ALL PEOPLE AS EXTENSIONS OF HIMSELF, WHICH IS CALLED BEING CHRISTLIKE, BECAUSE THAT'S LITERALLY WHAT HE SAW.

FREUD WAS A BIG COCAINE USER, AND COINED "NARCISSIST" AND IT WAS NEVER USED AS WIDELY AS IT IS TODAY, I FIND IT CONSTANTLY USED (LIKE MOST PSYCHOLOGICAL TERMS) BY PEOPLE WHO ONLY STUDY THE PART OF PSYCHOLOGY THAT'S RELEVANT TO WHO THEY'RE TRYING TO CHANGE. *EYE ROLL*. ONE OF HIS FEW FEMALE STUDENTS, LOU ANDREAS SALOME POINTED OUT THAT THERE WAS A BIT OF COKE LOGIC IN THE DIAGNOSIS OF THE NARCISSIST. FOR THOSE OF YOU WHO HAVEN'T ALSO SPENT A DECADE OR SO UNDER THE ILLUSION THAT "COCAINE SOBERS YOU UP", COKE LOGIC GETS FEROCIOUSLY LINEAR AND YOU CAN FIND YOURSELF FURIOUSLY INSISTING THE 1 + THE 1 EQUALS THE 2 DON'T YOU SEE?!?

WHEN SHE EXPLAINED THE DUAL FUNCTION OF NARCISSISM TO HIM, HE NOT ONLY TOOK IT TO HEART AND PEN, BUT INSTANTLY ENTRUSTED THE PSYCHOANALYSIS OF HIS BELOVED DAUGHTER AND PROTEGE, ANNA, TO LOU, WHICH SHE CONTINUED FOR MANY YEARS. BECAUSE SHE HAD A POINT.

AS YOU BECOME MORE FASCINATED WITH WHO YOU ARE AKA SELF HELP, AND PERSONAL DEVELOPMENT PEOPLE WILL DEFINITELY CALL YOU A NARCISSIST AND MUCH WORSE THINGS. BUT AT LEAST NOW YOU'LL BE ABLE TO ENLIGHTEN THEM ON SOMETHING THAT'S REMAINED AT THE CUTTING EDGE OF PSYCHOANALYSIS FOR OVER A CENTURY.

I'M A BITCH, TRUTHFULLY, WITH A "GET MONEY" ATTITUDE LACKING IN MANY SPIRITUAL COMMUNITIES. SINCE I'M A BIT OF A LOUD EXAMPLE OF "NARCISISSM IS OK" I'LL INCLUDE A QUOTE FROM MY FAVORITE DO-NO-WRONG AUTHOR AND RENUNCIATE, RAM DASS ON THE NEXT PAGE.

SEE YOU FOR OUR FIRST LESSON

Q: COULD YOU SUM UP THE BASIC MESSAGE OF YOUR LIFE?

RAM DASS: *I WOULD SAY THAT THE THRUST OF MY LIFE HAS BEEN INITIALLY ABOUT GETTING FREE, AND THEN REALIZING THAT MY FREEDOM IS NOT INDEPENDENT OF EVERYBODY ELSE. THEN I AM ARRIVING AT THAT CIRCLE WHERE ONE WORKS ON ONESELF AS A GIFT TO OTHER PEOPLE SO THAT ONE DOESN'T CREATE MORE SUFFERING. I HELP PEOPLE AS A WORK ON MYSELF AND I WORK ON MYSELF TO HELP PEOPLE.*

I'VE BEEN PERFECTING THAT CIRCLE FOR THIRTY YEARS. IT'S KARMA YOGA. DO WHAT YOU CAN ON THIS PLANE TO RELIEVE SUFFERING BY CONSTANTLY WORKING ON YOURSELF TO BE AN INSTRUMENT FOR THE CESSATION OF SUFFERING. TO ME, THAT'S WHAT THE EMERGING GAME IS ALL ABOUT.

let's get started..

THE FUNCTION OF A LAUNCH SHOULD BE TO PREPARE YOUR CLIENT FOR THE WORK AHEAD. THE FUNCTION OF A PRIMER IS TO CREATE A BETTER SURFACE FOR THE INTENDED SUBSTANCE TO ADHERE TO, WHETHER IT'S PAINT, MAKEUP, OR EDUCATION. THIS IS A PRIMER ON AUTHENTICITY AND MARKETING. A LAUNCH IS A PRIMER.

BEFORE WE CAN GET STARTED, WE HAVE TO GET RID OF ONE CORE BELIEF YOU HAVE THAT IS FUCKING UP THE REST OF YOUR GAME, AND THAT IS THE NOTION THAT "SELLING IS BAD" OR "SELLING IS ANNOYING". BOTH ARE EQUALLY TOXIC, AND EACH AS EFFECTIVE AT BLOCKING YOU FROM DOING WHAT MUST BE DONE. I WANT TO MOVE HARD AND FAST IN THIS WORKSHOP, AND YOU WILL BEGIN SELLING AS SOON AS WE BEGIN, BASICALLY.

AT POINT THREE, THE FOURTH SET OF LECTURES IN THIS WORKSHOP, YOU WILL INEVITABLY TELL ME THAT THIS BLOCK HAS REARED ITS UGLY HEAD AGAIN, BUT IT MUSTN'T BE YOUR FIRST TIME WRANGLING IT. WE HAVE SHIT TO DO.

YOU CAME HERE TO EARTH TO DO A THING. PLAIN AND SIMPLE. IF YOU DON'T ACCOMPLISH THE THING YOU CAME HERE TO DO, YOU ARE GOING TO REPEAT THIS LIFE UNTIL YOU GET IT DONE. SAME BIRTHDAY, SAME PARENTS, SAME SHIT, DIFFERENT ROUND.

DOING THE THING INVOLVES BEING PERSONALLY RESPONSIBLE FOR MAKING THE WORLD AWARE OF THE VALUE OF THIS THING YOU ARE DOING. YOU NEED TO STOP ANY KIND OF "I NEED AN AGENT." , "I NEED A HYPEBEAST", "I NEED TO BE DISCOVERED." SHIT NOW. ANYTIME YOU SAY "I NEED" YOU'RE DESCRIBING A DORMANT TALENT WITHIN YOURSELF THAT MUST BE ACTIVATED. NO ONE IS COMING TO SAVE YOU, PERIOD. YOU NEED TO REPRESENT YOURSELF. YOU NEED TO HYPE YOUR TALENTS UP. YOU NEED TO PUT YOURSELF IN POSITIONS WHERE PEOPLE CAN DISCOVER YOUR WORK.

Putting yourself in a position where people can discover your work is called marketing.

THERE ARE PLENTY OF SUPREMELY TALENTED AUTHORS OUT THERE WHO HAVE NEVER PUBLISHED A MANUSCRIPT. PLENTY OF TALENTED PAINTERS THAT HAVE NEVER SOLD A PIECE.

THE FAME EQUATION HAS CHANGED. IT USED TO BE THAT YOU COULD PAY A RECORD LABEL OR A PUBLISHING COMPANY TO MAKE YOU FAMOUS. YOU COULD STAY YOUR SHY, SHRINKING, UNACTIVATED, SELF. YOU COULD CONTINUE FONDLING YOUR EGO IN PERPETUAL "HERMIT MODE", STACKING UP CREATIVE WORK AND HIRING OTHER PEOPLE TO HELP YOU GET IT OUT IN THE WORLD.

A TEACHER OF MINE GOT A PUBLISHING DEAL WITH SIMON AND SCHUSTER FOR HER FIRST BOOK. SHE HAD AN AUDIENCE OF 50K ON INSTAGRAM AT THE TIME, AND CELEBRITY CLIENTELE. SHE HIRED AN EXTREMELY EXPENSIVE PUBLICIST TO HELP WITH THE LAUNCH OF THE BOOK. SHE DID HER AFFIRMATIONS EVERY SINGLE DAY. 15 REPS, WRITTEN IN A JOURNAL, DAILY. HER AIM? A NEW YORK TIMES BESTSELLER, WHICH IS SELLING 5000 COPIES IN THE FIRST WEEK. WITH THE COMBINATION OF HER PUBLICIST AND PUBLISHER, HER SPIRITUAL TOOLS, AS WELL AS THE UNIQUE NATURE OF HER BOOK, WHICH WAS TRULY A FIRST IN ITS FIELD, SHE WAS CERTAIN IT WOULD BE AN OUT OF THE BALL-PARK SUCCESS.

WHEN IT CAME TO PERSONAL MARKETING, SHE LET SOMEONE ELSE HANDLE IT FOR HER. SHE WOULD SHOW UP AND PROMOTE THE BOOK WHEN SHE WAS INSTRUCTED TO. HER SALES? 700 COPIES.

ANOTHER EXAMPLE I LOVE, BECAUSE THE INVESTMENT WAS MORE COSTLY, IS TOM O'NEILL.

TOM O'NEILL WROTE A REALLY AMAZING BOOK CALLED CHAOS: CHARLES MANSON, THE CIA, AND THE SECRET HISTORY OF THE SIXTIES. IT TOOK HIM 20 YEARS, DURING WHICH HE WAS UNABLE TO ACCOMPLISH MUCH ELSE. MUCH OF IT WAS WRITTEN FROM HIS PARENTS BASEMENT. IT STARTED AS AN ARTICLE FOR A MAGAZINE, AND WHEN IT MOVED INTO BOOK FORMAT IT WAS PICKED UP BY LITTLE, BROWN AND COMPANY.

WHEN THE BOOK WAS FINALLY RELEASED IN 2019, IT TANKED. IT SOLD UNDER A THOUSAND COPIES. THIS IS NOT A VERY BIG PAYCHECK FOR AN AUTHOR. IF YOU SOLD 5000 COPIES FOR $30 APIECE, THE TOTAL SALES WOULD BE 150K. THE AUTHOR'S PAYCHECK WOULD BE AROUND $11K, OR 7.5%. HOWEVER, IF YOU RECEIVED AN 11K BOOK ADVANCE, YOU WOULD ONLY START GETTING CHECKS ONCE YOU PAID BACK THE ADVANCE, DEDUCTED FROM YOUR ROYALTIES, OF COURSE. FOR A THOUSAND COPIES, THAT'S LESS THAN $750.

$750 for two decades of work

THE ONLY REASON I KNOW ABOUT THIS BOOK AT ALL, THE ONLY REASON ANYONE DOES IS BECAUSE JOE ROGAN SOMEHOW GOT AHOLD OF IT. IF YOU'VE EVER LISTENED TO ANY LONG-FORM PODCAST, YOU KNOW THAT YOU CAN'T REALLY BE GUARDED ABOUT WHAT YOU WILL AND WILL NOT TALK ABOUT, BECAUSE ANYTHING COMES UP. AUTHENTICITY IS A REQUIREMENT FOR THAT LEVEL OF PRESS, AND PEOPLE WHO ARE *UNCONSCIOUSLY* AFRAID OF PRESS ARE USUALLY THIS WAY BECAUSE OF A FEAR OF WHO WILL COME OUT WHEN THEY'RE ON CAMERA FOR THAT LONG. THAT WAS HIM PROMOTING HIMSELF. HIS PUBLISHER DIDN'T DO THAT FOR HIM, NOR DID ANY PUBLICIST.

AFTER HE WENT ON THE JRE, HIS BOOKS WERE SOLD OUT FOR WEEKS, AND BOY, AM I HAPPY THAT WAS THE CASE.

I WAS INTRODUCED TO THE BOOK BECAUSE MY HUSBAND HAD LISTENED TO THE PODCAST AND BOUGHT THE BOOK, AND HE MENTIONED TO ME THAT MY MOM'S STORY OF JOINING THE CHILDREN OF GOD SOUNDED A LOT LIKE ANOTHER FRIEND'S MOM'S STORY OF JOINING THE CHILDREN OF GOD. A DRUG RAID SCARE TURNED INTO A "COME TO JESUS" EPIPHANY ON THE BEACH, AND NEXT THING THEY KNEW, THEY HAD JOINED A CULT THAT WENT FROM CHASTE, EVANGELICAL CHRISTIAN CAMP TO RELIGIOUS EXTREMIST SEX CULT WITH A SPOTLIGHT FOR PEDOPHILIA IN LESS THAN 5 YEARS.

MAKING THE PSYCHOLOGICAL SHIFT FROM EVANGELICAL CHRISTIAN TO HAVING PHOTOGRAPHS OF YOU MOLESTING CHILDREN DURING ORGIES (HER MOM, NOT MINE) PUBLISHED AND DISTRIBUTED IN MANUALS CULT-WIDE, IS NOT AN EASY ONE. I DIDN'T WANT TO HEAR ANY OF HIS THEORIES ABOUT WHY MY PARENTS MIGHT HAVE JOINED A CULT. WHAT DID HE KNOW?

BUT THE MESSAGE OF THE BOOK HAD GOTTEN TO HIM. A TRANSITION LIKE THAT IS EASIER WHEN THERE IS GOVERNMENT INVOLVEMENT. HAD THIS BOOK NOT GARNERED MAINSTREAM SUCCESS VIA TOM O'NEILL'S PERSONAL PROMOTION, I WOULD HAVE NEVER BEEN ABLE TO FIND CLOSURE AROUND A QUESTION I HAD BEEN TRYING TO ANSWER FOR 25 YEARS:

why did my parents join a pedophile doomsday cult?

YOUR ART CAN HAVE A MOST UNEXPECTED IMPACT. LIKE HELPING ME SEE A PERSPECTIVE WHERE MAYBE MY PARENTS WEREN'T MALICIOUS IDIOTS.

JUST WRONG PLACE, WRONG TIME, WRONG CUP.

FOR OUR FINAL EXAMPLE WE HAVE GABBY BERNSTEIN, A NEW YORK-BASED SPIRITUAL TEACHER, WHO WAS THE FIRST SELF HELP AUTHOR I EVER READ. HER BOOK WAS GIVEN FREE WHEN I SIGNED UP FOR NUTRITION SCHOOL IN 2011. SHE HAS WRITTEN NINE BOOKS AND ALL OF THEM HAVE BEEN BESTSELLERS, ONE OF THEM WAS EVEN THE #1 NEW YORK TIMES BESTSELLER, WHICH MEANS IT SOLD MORE COPIES THAN ANY OTHER BOOK ON THAT LIST.

I HAVE BEEN ON GABBY'S MAILING LIST SINCE 2011, SO I SEE THE WAY SHE SELF PROMOTES AND MAKES HER BOOKS BESTSELLERS FROM THE VERY BEGINNING. I'VE TAKEN FOUR OF HER COURSES, AROUND 5K WORTH OF WORK, AND WHAT I HAVE LEARNED FROM OBSERVING HER PRACTICE SALES AND LAUNCHING IS MORE VALUABLE THAN ANY FORMAL WORKSHOP THAT SHE SELLS. SHE ALSO CANNOT SPELL BY HER OWN ADMISSION, AND SHE'S A MULTIPLE BESTSELLING AUTHOR.

TO BE A NEW YORK TIMES BESTSELLER, YOU NEED 5000 SALES IN THE FIRST WEEK TO QUALIFY, BUT WHAT DOES IT *ACTUALLY* MEAN WHEN A SELF-HELP AUTHOR SELLS 5000 COPIES? WHY IS THAT IMPORTANT?

IT MEANS THEY REACHED A MINIMUM OF 5,000 PEOPLE. 5000 PEOPLE WHO WILL NO LONGER STRUGGLE WITH THE TOPIC THE BOOK IS WRITTEN ON. 5000 PEOPLE WHO WILL HAND THAT BOOK OFF TO 5000 MORE PEOPLE, CREATING A MASSIVE RIPPLE EFFECT IN THE WORLD. 5000 PEOPLE WHO WILL PROBABLY HAVE THREE CONVERSATIONS MINIMUM ABOUT THE IMPACT THE BOOK HAD ON THEM IN THEIR LIFETIME. IF ONE OF THESE PEOPLE HAS A WIDE SOCIAL MEDIA INFLUENCE, MAYBE 1M PEOPLE, THAT'S POTENTIALLY ONE MILLION MORE PEOPLE HEALED BECAUSE THE AUTHOR GOT OVER THE "SELLING IS BAD, SELLING IS ANNOYING" STORY THAT SO MANY CREATORS HAVE.

If the creation serves, the creator deserves.
You serve, you deserve.
The End.

TO GO EVEN DEEPER, THE AMAZON BESTSELLER LIST HAS BEEN HOTTER THAN THE NYT BESTSELLER LIST FOR SEVERAL YEARS. BECAUSE, AFTER SEVERAL AUTHOR DISPUTES, THE NYT BESTSELLER LIST IS NOW PUBLICLY KNOWN AS "EDITORIAL CONTENT", WHICH MEANS THEY CHOOSE WHO GOES ON IT, REGARDLESS OF BOOK SALES. THEY'RE KNOWN FOR REMOVING UNKNOWN OR FIRST TIME AUTHORS, WHICH IS SHIT BECAUSE BREAKTHROUGH AUTHORS ARE REALLY WHO YOU WANT TO SEE ON THAT LIST. IT'S THE ORIGINAL SOURCE OF BOOK VIRALITY.

I came across an author on TikTok

WHO WRITES YOUNG ADULT EROTIC FICTION. I WAS GOBSMACKED BY HER MARKETING STYLE. IT WAS ABSOLUTELY RIVETING, COMPLETELY AUTHENTIC, AND SUSTAINABLE. THIS WOMAN HAD FOUND A WAY OF PROMOTING HER MANY BOOKS FROM THE POV OF ONE OF THE MAIN CHARACTERS, FOR EXAMPLE SHARING SCREENSHOTS OF "HER" DRUNK TEXTING HER THERAPIST, AND IT GETTING SPICY. IT WAS FUN, FRESH, HOT, AND REALLY MADE YOU WANT TO BUY HER BOOK. SHE POSTED A VIDEO SHORTLY AFTERWARDS THANKING TIKTOK FOR MAKING HER POST VIRAL AND MAKING BOOK THE #1 AMAZON BESTSELLER.

WHEN YOU SELF PUBLISH, USING AMAZON KDP, YOU KEEP 60% OF ROYALTIES, PAID OUT 60 DAYS FROM PURCHASE DATE, AND THEY TAKE 40% FOR ALL PRINTING, RETURNS, AND DISTRIBUTION. THE BOOKS ARE DROP-SHIPPED, SO THERE IS NO NEED TO HOLD INVENTORY IN A WAREHOUSE OR USE A MIDDLEMAN LIKE A LITERARY AGENT. SHIPPING COSTS ALONE MAKE UP 40% OF EVERY PHYSICAL ITEM'S COST OF PRODUCTION, SO THAT'S PRETTY CHEAP. IF THIS WOMAN SOLD, LET'S SAY, 2000 COPIES AT $15 PER BOOK, WHICH IS CONSERVATIVE, THAT'S $18,000 DIRECT TO HER POCKETS OFF OF ONE TIKTOK VIDEO IN ONE DAY.

$18,000 in one day

$18,000+ BECAUSE SHE ADMITTED THAT NO ONE WAS COMING TO SAVE HER AND JUST DID IT HER DAMN SELF. $18,000+ BECAUSE SHE KNEW HOW TO MARKET HERSELF. MOST SELF PUBLISHED AUTHORS SELL LESS THAN 150 COPIES, BECAUSE THEY REFUSE TO LEARN HOW TO MARKET.

I USE THE PUBLISHING INDUSTRY AS AN EXAMPLE NOT JUST BECAUSE I'M BUILDING MY OWN PUBLISHING COMPANY, ONAMI HOUSE, BUT BECAUSE BOOKS ARE SO MUCH HARDER TO GET EXCITED ABOUT SELLING THAN ANYTHING ELSE.

I USE THE PUBLISHING INDUSTRY AS AN EXAMPLE NOT JUST BECAUSE I'M BUILDING MY OWN PUBLISHING COMPANY, ONAMI HOUSE, BUT BECAUSE BOOKS ARE SO MUCH HARDER TO GET EXCITED ABOUT SELLING THAN ANYTHING ELSE.

WHY?

BECAUSE BOOKS TAKE A LONG ASS TIME TO WRITE, AND WHEN YOU ARE DONE WITH THEM IT FEELS LIKE THEY'RE DONE WITH YOU TOO. AFTER BEING IMMERSED IN THAT WORLD NON STOP, YOU NEVER WANT TO LOOK AT THE FUCKING THING AGAIN. YOU'RE ON TO THE NEXT BOOK AND IT WOULD BE SO NICE IF YOU COULD HERMIT DOWN AND JUST IMMERSE YOURSELF IN THE WRITING OF THE NEXT BOOK FULLY WITHOUT HAVING TO GET UP THERE AND READ CHAPTERS YOU'VE WRITTEN AND SELL THE SAME STORY THAT'S BEEN CHAFING THE CREATIVE BANE FOR THE LAST YEAR/S OF YOUR LIFE.

Promoting the same exact product you finished years ago and don't quite resonate with now can feel exhausting.

A LOT OF TIMES THE BOOK DOESN'T COME OUT FOR A YEAR OR TWO AFTER IT'S BEEN WRITTEN, SO IT'S VERY OLD NEWS TO YOU.

 WRITING IS THE CREATIVE MODALITY THAT TAKES UP THE MOST OF YOUR TIME, AND USUALLY A BOOK HAS A BIG SPLASH WHEN IT LAUNCHES AND THEN DISAPPEARS INTO OBLIVION UNLESS IT GOES ON INTO MOVIEDOM.

THE PUBLISHING COMPANY DOESN'T OFTEN RELAUNCH UNLESS A BOOK WAS CRAZY SUCCESSFUL, SO YOU HAVE NO REAL SURGE IN SALES OUTSIDE OF THE INITIAL SPLASH. THAT IS SO UNFAIR AFTER SUCH HARD WORK, BUT UNFORTUNATELY IN THE MEDIA BUSINESS, THIS IS JUST HOW IT IS. MOVIES PREMIERE IN THEATERS, PREMIERE ON STREAMING, AND THEN IT'S DONE. ALBUMS COME AND GO. YOU GET STUCK IN THE RAT RACE OF HAVING TO MAKE A WHOLE NEW ART PIECE EVERY TIME YOU WANT MONEY.

NO RAPPER BECAME A BILLIONAIRE FROM ALBUMS. PRESS AND RADIO CAN PROMOTE ALBUMS, BUT IT'S ULTIMATELY NOT UP TO YOU TO MAKE SOMETHING A HIT, NO MATTER HOW FAMOUS YOU ARE. DON'T GET ME STARTED ON THE UNFAIRNESS OF RECORD CONTRACTS.

JAY Z BECAME A BILLIONAIRE WITH ROCAWEAR, YE WITH YEEZY, RIHANNA WITH FENTY. THEY FOUND A WAY TO AUTHENTICALLY PROMOTE 24/7, SIMPLY BY USING THE PRODUCTS THEY MADE BECAUSE THEY ABSOLUTELY BELIEVED IN THEM. THEY DIVERSIFIED WITHIN INDUSTRIES THEY WERE PASSIONATE ABOUT, MAKING PRODUCTS AT A PRICE POINT WHERE THEIR CUSTOMER COULD FEEL AT THE SAME LEVEL AS THEIR IDOL BY USING THE PRODUCT. THIS IS WHAT WE'RE GOING FOR WITH YOU. A WAY YOU CAN BE MARKETING, AUTHENTICALLY, ALL THE TIME, AS EASILY AS WEARING YOUR OWN MAKEUP OR YOUR OWN T-SHIRT.

WHEN YOU HAVE HIRED PEOPLE TO DO YOUR MARKETING FOR YOU, YOU NO LONGER HAVE THE ABILITY TO FINANCIALLY TAP *YOUR* AUDIENCE THAT YOU BUILT THROUGH BLOOD, SWEAT, AND TEARS. IT IS THE WORST POSSIBLE MIDDLEMAN TO HIRE, AND DO NOT EVEN THINK ABOUT BRINGING AI IN TO DO IT FOR YOU.

ANY FACULTY YOU HIRE AI FOR IS A FACULTY YOU WILL LOSE THROUGH DISUSE. WHEN PEOPLE NOTICE THE LACK OF AUTHENTICITY AND CREATIVITY IN YOUR SALES PITCH, WHICH IS THE MARK OF AI OR GETTING SOMEONE TO DO IT FOR YOU, THEY'LL STOP BUYING. YOU WILL NOT BE ABLE TO RESUSCITATE YOUR BUSINESS THAT SOMETHING "BETTER AT MARKETING" THAN YOU KILLED, BECAUSE IF YOU DO NOT USE YOUR INHERENT ABILITY TO MARKET, YOU WILL MOST CERTAINLY LOSE IT. IT IS A SPIRITUAL FACULTY.

If you outsource your marketing, you no longer have the ability to make your own money.

THE MYTH IS THAT YOU'LL BE BAD AT IT, JUST LIKE PARENTS WHO ARE AFRAID THEY WILL FUCK UP THEIR CHILDREN'S EDUCATION IF THEY DO IT THEMSELVES. NOTHING COULD BE FURTHER THAN THE TRUTH. AS A BUSINESS OWNER, AND PARENT, NO ONE CARES MORE THAN YOU. EVERY MOMENT THE CHILD SPENDS WITH YOU IS EDUCATIONAL BECAUSE YOU CARE THE MOST. EVERY MOMENT FOR YOU IS EDUCATIONAL BECAUSE IT'S DATA YOU RETAIN ON HOW YOUR CHILD LEARNS. YOU ALWAYS KNOW WHAT'S BEEN COVERED, AND WHAT IS STILL NEW TO UNCOVER. YOU LEARN AS YOU GO ALONG, OFTENTIMES TOGETHER WITH YOUR CHILD. WHEN YOU OUTSOURCE THIS, YOU PAY PEOPLE TO CARE. YOU PAY FOR MORE ATTENTION ON YOUR KIDS. NOT FOR A STRONGER CURRICULUM. NOT FOR MORE MARKETING TALENT. FOR ATTENTION. FOR TUTORS AND TWENTY-SOMETHINGS WHO **DO** HAVE THE GALL TO SAY THEY ARE EXPERTS, YOU WILL PAY AND PAY AND PAY TO HAVE THEM RETAIN THE DATA ON YOUR COMPANY.

EVEN ON A TUTOR'S BEST DAY, THEY DON'T KNOW OR CARE ABOUT ONE OF THEIR 300 JOBS AS MUCH AS YOU CARE ABOUT YOUR CHILD.

EVEN ON A MARKETING EXEC'S BEST DAY THEY DO NOT KNOW THE COMPANY OR CARE ABOUT THE COMPANY AS MUCH AS YOU CARE ABOUT YOUR BUSINESS.

NO ONE CAN DO IT BETTER THAN YOU.

Your insecurity about your ability to do something that isn't even that hard, is costing you hundreds of thousands of dollars at the low end.

IT'S KEEPING YOU WEAK AND REDUCING YOUR CHILD'S CHANCES FOR A TRULY SPECIALIZED EDUCATION. IT'S KEEPING YOU WEAK AND HURTING YOUR BUSINESS.

IT'S TIME TO GROW A SET.

Here's exactly how you start to grow your marketing skills:

THERE IS AN EASY WAY TO DO THINGS, AND A HARD WAY TO DO THINGS. THE EASY WAY IS THE ALIGNED WAY. THE ALIGNED WAY IS THE AUTHENTIC WAY

WHEN YOU DO THINGS IN AN ALIGNED WAY, EVERYTHING FLOWS THROUGH YOU. YOU JUST SHOW UP WHEN YOU'RE PROMPTED, AND LIVE YOUR LIFE THE REST OF THE TIME. MY BUSINESS ONLY COSTS ME MORE THAN TWO HOURS A DAY WHEN I'M ACTIVELY WRITING BOOKS, WHICH IS WHEN I WAKE UP EARLY (3:28 AM PRESENTLY, NO ALARM) TO WRITE FOR AN ADDITIONAL TWO HOURS IN SILENCE BEFORE GOING BACK TO BED.

IT FEELS EASY. IT FEELS FUN. AND YOU PROBABLY ALREADY KNOW HOW TO DO THIS.

THE PROBLEM IS, YOU DON'T TRUST IT. YOU DON'T TRUST THAT SOMETHING SO EASY, SO RIGHT, LIKE FREESCHOOLING, COULD BE WORKING "GOOD ENOUGH". YOU HAVE THIS INSECURITY THAT YOU'RE FUCKING IT UP. THAT YOU NEED TO FAKE IT. THAT YOU NEED TO MAKE IT HARD TO BE "LEGIT". WHEN YOU GO INTO THIS MISALIGNED WAY OF THINKING, IT CAN GO ON ENDLESSLY. THE GOOD NEWS IS THAT ALIGNMENT IS HOME, AND FALLING OUT OF ALIGNMENT IS THE STRANGER. THE STRANGER CAN ALWAYS LEAVE, AND YOU CAN ALWAYS RETURN HOME.

THE SECOND PROBLEM IS, ALIGNMENT IS SUBJECTIVE. EVEN THOUGH WE ARE ALL IN THE SAME FLOW, WHAT IS RIGHT FOR ME IS NOT LIKELY RIGHT FOR YOU. ME BEING AUTHENTIC LIKE ME WILL NOT SHOW YOU HOW TO BE AUTHENTIC LIKE YOU, ONLY THAT IT IS OKAY TO BE AUTHENTIC.

THIS IS WHY THIS BOOK YOU'RE HOLDING IN YOUR HANDS IS A GROUNDBREAKER. IT'S AN OBJECTIVE PATH TO ALIGNED MARKETING. AN OBJECTIVE PATH TO AUTHENTICITY.

we track objective authenticity in three ways:

1.)Human Design
2.) The Enneagram
3.) Questions

HUMAN DESIGN GIVES US THE ABILITY TO SEE WHAT EVERY INDIVIDUAL'S BLUEPRINT IS, AND EXACTLY WHERE AND HOW THEY SHOULD LEAN INTO THIS FOR THE MAXIMUM POSSIBLE RESULTS. NO MATTER WHO THE PERSON IS, IF THEY GO TO THEIR CHART AND LOOK AT THIS ASPECT OF THEMSELVES, THEY WILL FIND THE ANSWER, AND I WILL SHOW YOU HOW TO IMPLEMENT IT.

THE ENNEAGRAM IS AN ESOTERIC SYMBOL THAT SHOWS HOW THREE FUNDAMENTAL LAWS OF CREATION WORK HARMONIOUSLY TO CREATE ALL THINGS. IT IS THE MASTER OF ALL SYSTEMS, AND ALLOWS THE USER TO SEE A SYSTEMIC APPROACH TO ANY TASK, GREAT OR SMALL. IT ELIMINATES ANY UNNECESSARY ACTIVITIES, LEAVING ONLY THE NECESSARY ACTION.

THE UPSIDE OF ENNEAGRAM-BASED WORK IS THAT IT GUARANTEES RESULTS IF EVERY STEP IS TAKEN. THERE IS NO FASTER WAY, AND IT WORKS OBJECTIVELY, MEANING, FOR ALL PEOPLE. IT DOES NOT BREAK, IT DOES NOT FAIL, AND IT IS NOT ONLY REUSABLE, IT GETS STRONGER EVERY TIME. THE DOWNSIDE OF THIS IS THAT EVERY STEP MUST BE COMPLETED, AND WHEN IT'S HARD, YOU HAVE TO WORK VERY HARD NOT TO GIVE UP AT SPECIFIC TIMES, WHICH I ALWAYS DISCLOSE TO YOU. (SHORT ANSWER: WHEREVER TRIANGLE POINTS ARE.)

THE STRUCTURE OF THIS BOOK, OF THE WORKSHOP, OF THE WORK ITSELF IS ALL BACKED UP ONTO THE ENNEAGRAM, SO YOU WILL ACHIEVE THE DESIRED RESULT. YOU DO THE WORK, YOU GET THE RESULT.

I AM CURRENTLY THE ONLY LIVING PERSON TEACHING THE ENNEAGRAM AS AN ESOTERIC FORMULA, NOT A PERSONALITY TEST.

QUESTIONS MEAN I DON'T TELL YOU HOW TO BE YOU, I ASK YOU, SO YOU CAN TELL YOU, AND ASK OTHERS.

WHAT IS
YOUR TRUTH?

WHO'S NOT
GOING TO
LIKE IT?

WHO ARE
YOU?

CAN
YOU
TURN
BACK?

WHAT
ARE
YOUR
GIFTS?

WHO
COULD
YOU BE?

DO YOU
TRUST
YOU?

WHAT IS
STOPPING
YOU? (TRAUMA)

WHAT IS
YOUR STORY?

*YOU CAN LEARN MORE ABOUT THE ENNEAGRAM IN MY
FREE EBOOK NINE LINES, WHICH IS ALSO AVAILABLE FREE
ON YOUR SAFEHOUSE GLOBAL APP. IT'S THE PRIMER FOR
THE FULL LENGTH ENNEAGRAM WORKSHOP*

Who am I?

YOU WOULDN'T TAKE A SCUBA DIVING LESSON FROM SOMEONE WHO HAD NEVER DONE IT BEFORE, SO I GUESS I'LL INTRODUCE MYSELF.

MY NAME IS ONAMI, BUT EVERYONE CALLS ME MAMI. THAT'S FINE WITH ME.

I GREW UP IN A REALLY FUCKED UP DOOMSDAY SEX CULT CALLED THE CHILDREN OF GOD, AND ESCAPED WHEN I WAS THIRTEEN YEARS OLD VIA A BOTCHED PILL SUICIDE ATTEMPT THAT GOT ME EXCOMMUNICATED BY MY OWN MOTHER.

BECAUSE OF THAT, **ALL I WANTED TO DO WAS BLEND IN** AND BE NORMAL. MY DAD HAD TAKEN OFF TO SOUTH AFRICA TO BE WITH A TRULY AWFUL WOMAN, TELLING MY 15 YEAR OLD OLDER BROTHER AND I THAT IF WE (I) COULD SAVE UP ENOUGH MONEY TO GET OUT THERE, WE COULD MEET UP WITH HIM ON A NEW CONTINENT.

WE RENTED A LIVING ROOM COUCH FOR $500 A MONTH WITH SOME EX-MEMBERS, AND EVERY DAY I WOULD GET DROPPED OFF TO GO STAND AT THE SWEET FACTORY IN THE MALL, OR AT RUBY'S IN SAN JUAN CAPISTRANO AND **SELL BALLOON ANIMALS FOR $1 A PIECE**. I HAD BEEN DOING THIS SINCE I WAS ABOUT NINE YEARS OLD, AND AT LEAST AS A THIRTEEN YEAR OLD ADULT I DIDN'T HAVE TO DRESS UP LIKE A CLOWN TO DO IT. MY BROTHER STAYED HOME WATCHING TV.

IT WAS INCREMENTALLY DAWNING ON ME THAT NO ONE ELSE IN THE REAL WORLD BELIEVED THAT THE ENDTIME WAS COMING, OR WAS CURRENTLY HAPPENING. I HAD NEVER LISTENED TO MUSIC, WATCHED TV, OR READ A MAGAZINE. I HAD NEVER BEEN TO SCHOOL OR HAD A CONVERSATION ABOVE SMALL TALK WITH ANYONE OUTSIDE OF THE CULT. **I WAS TERRIFIED, ABSOLUTELY TERRIFIED THAT PEOPLE WOULD FIND OUT ABOUT WHERE I HAD COME FROM AND THINK I WAS WEIRD**, SO I STUDIED PEOPLE OBSESSIVELY AND LEARNED HOW TO MIMIC THEIR WORDS AND BEHAVIORS SO I COULD LOOK NORMAL.

ON MUSHROOMS, ABOUT 5 YEARS LATER I REALIZED THAT EVERYTHING I WAS WAS NOT ME. I SAW HOW EVERYTHING I SAID AND DID HAD BEEN CO-OPTED FROM SOMEONE ELSE. THAT LITERALLY EVERYTHING ABOUT ME WASN'T ME. I WALKED LIKE HER, I TOLD HIS JOKES, I SAID HER CATCHPHRASE, I DANCED LIKE HER. **THERE WAS ABSOLUTELY NOT ONE AUTHENTIC THING ABOUT ME, AND I COULDN'T STOP.** THE WORST PART WAS THAT I DIDN'T EVEN LIKE A LOT OF THESE PEOPLE, BUT THEY WERE NORMAL. THAT WAS MY HIGHEST ASPIRATION. NORMAL.

IT TOOK FIFTEEN MORE YEARS OF FAKING IT UNTIL I WAS FORCED INTO AUTHENTICITY.

My life had taken a turn for the better

WHEN MY BEST FRIEND, SOMETIMES ROOMMATE, SOMETIMES LOVER OF TEN YEARS AND I GOT "OFFICIALLY" TOGETHER. SURE, HE WAS ADDICTED TO HEROIN BY THAT TIME, BUT I WAS CERTAIN I COULD REHAB HIM AND THAT WE WOULD OPEN A BAR AND HAVE THREE KIDS ONE DAY. MY HOPE BLURRED MY VISION, AND DISTRACTED ME FROM ACCEPTING HOW UNHAPPY HE WAS.

On September 9th, 2015 I had a dream that I came home and found him dead.

I HAD NEVER HAD A VIVID DREAM LIKE THAT BEFORE, BUT I WAS ABOUT 30 DAYS SOBER, "FOR HIM" WHILE HE WAS PRETENDING TO BE IN AN ABSTINENCE PROGRAM. SOBRIETY = DREAMS.

I WAS SHAKEN TO MY CORE. I TOLD HIS MOM, BROTHER, AND HIM ABOUT THE DREAM. THEY ALL TOLD ME TO SHAKE IT OFF. I COULDN'T. I MADE A POINT THAT DAY OF SEEING HIM FOR TWENTY MINUTES AS I WAS GOING TO WORK IN THE BAR, AND HE WAS LEAVING HIS CONSTRUCTION JOB. HE LOOKED SO TIRED IN UNION SQUARE THAT DAY, EVEN A LITTLE DRUNK, BUT I DIDN'T ASK.

That night I came home at 2AM and found him dead

I SPENT 22 MINUTES RESUSCITATING HIS DEAD BODY WHILE THE EMT'S CIRCLED THE NEIGHBORHOOD, LOOKING FOR OUR HOME.

I WAS OUT OF BODY THE ENTIRE TIME, AND CAME BACK TO EARTH FOR A DOSE OF SHOCK AND TRAUMA WHEN THE EMT TOLD ME HE HAD BEEN DEAD OF A SPEEDBALL FOR FOUR HOURS.

AFTER THAT, **I WAS TOO EXHAUSTED TO FAKE IT ANYMORE**. I COULDN'T EVER GO BACK TO MY JOB AND FAKE HAPPY WHILE POURING BOUGIE LOSERS VODKA SODAS. I COULDN'T EVER GO BACK TO MY APARTMENT AND PRETEND LIKE IT DIDN'T REEK OF BODY BAGS AND DEATH. I COULDN'T EVER PRETEND LIKE THE SUPERNATURAL DIDN'T EXIST, AND I COULDN'T KEEP MY MOUTH SHUT ABOUT IT.

WHILE LIVING AT HIS MOM'S HOUSE FOR A COUPLE OF WEEKS, PLANNING HIS MEMORIAL AND FIGURING OUT MY NEXT MOVE, I STARTED SENDING NEWSLETTERS TO MY 24 PERSON NEWSLETTER LIST. I WAS THE ONLY SOBER PERSON DURING A FULL IRISH BEREAVEMENT, AND I HAD AN OBE DURING HIS RESUSCITATION THAT MADE ME UNDERSTAND WHY IT HAD TO HAPPEN, SO I WAS **HAVING A VERY DIFFERENT EXPERIENCE THAN EVERYONE ELSE**. I HAD TO TALK TO SOMEONE, SO I STARTED SENDING A NEWSLETTER ALMOST DAILY, DESCRIBING WHERE I WAS AT AND WHAT I WAS LEARNING.

I DIDN'T "OFFICIALLY PIVOT" FROM YOGA AND HEALTH COACHING TO SPIRITUAL TEACHING. I JUST STARTED SHARING FROM MY PRESENT MOMENT AS OPPOSED TO FROM WHERE I FELT LIKE I WAS A PROFESSIONAL. I DIDN'T KNOW IT AT THE TIME, BUT **THIS WAS MY FIRST STEP TOWARDS MARKETING FROM MY DESIGN, AND BRINGING MY AUTHENTIC VOICE TO THE MIX.**

I **LEFT ON A ONE WAY TICKET TO THAILAND** THAT MY SISTER PAID FOR, WITH 3K FROM A 5K GO FUND ME THAT I KEPT THE CASH FOR INSTEAD OF PAYING OFF THE DEBT I ACCRUED MOVING US INTO A NEW APARTMENT THAT HE DIED 28 DAYS INTO LIVING IN. THE OTHER 2K WENT TOWARDS MY FIRST BUSINESS AND MARKETING COURSE EVER, GABBY BERNSTEIN'S SPIRIT JUNKIE MASTERCLASS.

I struggled

FOR THE FIRST TWO YEARS IN BUSINESS FOR MANY
REASONS, BUT THE MAIN FACTORS WERE:

1. ONLY SELLING 1:1 COACHING
2. NOT KNOWING WHAT LAUNCHING
   WAS OR UNDERSTANDING HOW TO DO IT
3. DEEP-ASS MONEY BLOCKS

I HAD NO PRODUCT LINE, AND THE CONVERSIONS FOR 1:1
COACHING WERE LOW, LIKE ALWAYS. I TELL PEOPLE NOT TO
FOCUS ON SELLING 1:1 ANYWAYS, BECAUSE IT'S MORE ABOUT
DEMONSTRATING WHAT YOU KNOW AND LESS ABOUT LETTING
PEOPLE KNOW YOU HAVE SPACES OPEN OVER AND OVER..
REACTIVE CUSTOMERS DON'T BUY 1:1 COACHING, SO ANY KIND
OF "TIME'S RUNNING OUT" SHIT DOESN'T WORK ON THEM. IT'S
AN INTUITIVE CUSTOMER THAT BUYS 1:1, WHEN IT'S THE RIGHT
MOMENT FOR *THEM*. SO DON'T FOCUS ON IT. BUILD SOMETHING
ELSE MORE PEOPLE CAN AFFORD, AND WE'LL TALK MORE ABOUT
CUSTOMER TYPES IN ANOTHER CHAPTER.

SO I BUILT A PRODUCT, BREAKING BROKE (FIRST VERSION) AND IT
DID *OKAY* WHEN I FIRST DEBUTED IT. I WAS TALKING ABOUT THE
WORKSHOP ALL THE TIME BECAUSE THAT WAS THE MAIN THING
GOING ON WITH ME AND THE EPIPHANY AROUND MONEY
BLOCKS WAS SO BIG I COULD NOT BELIEVE THE ENTREPRENEURIAL
ROAD WASN'T LOADED WITH BILLBOARDS SAYING "IT WILL NEVER
FUCKING WORK IF YOU HAVE MONEY BLOCKS". SO I DECIDED TO
MAKE THEM.

I DIDN'T UNDERSTAND LAUNCH STRATEGY, OR INCENTIVIZING,
SO THERE WASN'T REALLY ANY *REASON* WHY MY CUSTOMER
SHOULD PAY ME THEN AND NOT "AT SOME POINT", BUT I WAS
TALKING ABOUT IT A LOT WHILE IT WAS FRESH FOR ME, SO I SAW
SOME SALES.

You can learn about money blocks in my workshop Breaking Broke 2.0, how to scale a business in How to
Start a Business from Scratch, as well as Empress Academy, all included in your Safehouse subscription.

THEN THE SALES WORE OFF, AND I HAD BILLS AND CREDIT CARD MINIMUMS TO PAY. I HAD BLOCKS AROUND "SELLING IS BAD", SO I COULDN'T IMAGINE TALKING ABOUT MY MONEY WORKSHOP MORE, SO I JUST BUILT A NEW ONE. SPIRITUALITY 101. THE SAME THING HAPPENED.

WHEN IT WAS FIRST STARTING AND I WAS TALKING ABOUT IT A LOT, I SAW SOME SALES. THEN THEY WORE OFF AND WHAT, TIME TO MAKE A NEW WORKSHOP? I COULDN'T IMAGINE HAVING TO MAKE A NEW WORKSHOP EVERY TIME I WANTED NEW MONEY.

IT HAD TAKEN ME YEARS TO COMPILE THE BREAKING BROKE SYLLABUS, AND SPIRITUALITY 101. SPIRITUALITY 101 LAUNCHED IN MAY OF 2017. IN JULY OF 2017 I MET MY HUSBAND AND CELEBRATED BY GETTING PREGNANT THAT WEEKEND.

shit hit the fan when...

MY HUSBAND'S SPIRITUAL MENTOR TRIED TO RAPE ME AT A SWEAT LODGE, AND MY PLANS OF MOVING IN WITH HIM IMMEDIATELY CAPSIZED. INSTEAD OF REMOVING THE RAPIST, THEY REMOVED MY HUSBAND BECAUSE *CULTS* DON'T ALWAYS LOOK LIKE CULTS WHEN YOU JOIN THEM. MY HUSBAND WAS TEACHING CHILDREN MARTIAL ARTS AT THE TIME, FOR ABOUT $400 A WEEK BEFORE TAXES.

I HAD A FLEDGLING BUSINESS WHICH WAS ON TRACK FOR IT'S FIRST 40K YEAR, ALTHOUGH I WOULDN'T KNOW IT YET. THAT MEANT I HAD A BETTER CHANCE SUPPORTING OUR NEW FAMILY THAN HE DID. WE MEDITATED, PUT OUR HEADS TOGETHER, AND CAME UP WITH A PLAN. I SOLD EVERY DAY UNTIL I SIGNED FIVE CLIENTS AT 5K EACH FOR A TEACHER TRAINING.

AT THAT POINT IN 2017, PEOPLE ASSOCIATED ME WITH AUTHENTICITY ENOUGH TO BE TRAINED BY ME ON THE SAME TOPIC. WE SPENT 15K ON A DILAPIDATED TRUCK AND CAMPER, 3K ON SOME LAME ASS DENTAL WORK, AND THE REST QUICKLY DWINDLED DOWN THANKS TO THE FACT THAT THE TRUCK WAS COMPLETELY BROKEN. AFTER TWO MONTHS OF BEDREST FOR EXTREME MORNING SICKNESS, WE HIT THE ROAD WITH ABOUT 3K....

And no new money coming in.

IT WAS STRESSFUL. IT WAS SO STRESSFUL. THE TRUCK BROKE DOWN EVERY TWO WEEKS, AND WE ONLY FOUND OUT AT THE END OF THE ROAD TRIP, AND SO MANY MECHANICS, THAT IT ACTUALLY COULDN'T BE REPAIRED. AS OUR 3K BECAME LESS THAN $1000, I BEGGED AND PRAYED FOR A SOLUTION.

LIKE MOST ANSWERS TO MONEY PRAYERS, IT CAME IN THE FORM OF A BUSINESS BOOK, MY FIRST BUSINESS BOOK, LAUNCH, BY JEFF WALKER.

WE LISTENED TO THAT AUDIOBOOK ALL THROUGH COLORADO, UTAH, NEVADA, AND OREGON. WE FINISHED IT RIGHT AFTER ALMOST DYING IN TWO WHEEL DRIVE ON ON A MUDSLIDING HILL IN NEVADA CITY, CA, THE DAY AFTER I COMPLETED MY FIRST RELAUNCH FOR BREAKING BROKE. I HAD, OF COURSE, IMPLEMENTED THE SYSTEM IMMEDIATELY.

WE HAD JUST ARRIVED AT MY MOM'S HOUSE IN OCEANSIDE, CA WHEN THE NUMBERS STARTED ROLLING IN. **WE WERE DOWN TO $300 WHEN THE LAUNCH WRAPPED. IN A WEEK, WE MADE OVER $3500. CASH STRAIGHT TO THE BANK.**

THE NEXT LAUNCH WAS WHEELS:REINVENTED. 10K.

I wasn't aware there were other launch strategies, or that launch strategies become outdated at the same point as it becomes exhausting for you.

WE'LL DISCUSS THE JEFF WALKER PLF LAUNCH STRATEGY, AND MANY OTHERS IN FUCKLESS, BUT THE GIST OF IT IS THIS:

THREE PIECES OF LAUNCH CONTENT FOR A $2K PRODUCT, AND ABOUT 21 AUTOMATED EMAILS, FOLLOWED BY EIGHT OR NINE EMAILS IN THE LAST THREE DAYS. THAT WAS THE INDUSTRY STANDARD AT THE TIME. IF YOU'RE WONDERING WHY YOUR INBOX WAS SO COACH SPAMMED FROM 2015 TO 2020, THAT'S WHY. BUT, GOD BLESS ME, I SUPPORTED MY LITTLE FAMILY ON THAT SAME, TIRED, LAUNCH STRATEGY WHILE BREASTFEEDING AT NAPTIME. I TOOK US FROM 40K A YEAR TO 500K A YEAR IN JUST THREE YEARS ON THAT LAUNCH STRATEGY, BEFORE, SUDDENLY...

IT STOPPED WORKING.

I KEPT ATTEMPTING IT AND IT KEPT TANKING. PEOPLE WERE SICK OF IT. EMAILS WERE GOING UNREAD. MY GROWTH WAS STALLED, MY CHECKS WERE DRY.

When all your business tricks suddenly stop working, it's a sign you need to grow.

GROWTH NEVER HAPPENS IN ONE AREA OF LIFE ONLY, KIND OF LIKE YOU CAN'T GAIN WEIGHT IN YOUR ASS ONLY. YOU HAVE TO WORK THE INTERNAL, AND THE EXTERNAL. YOU HAVE TO KNOW THE THREE FACTORS OF LIFE, THE PHYSICAL, THE SPIRITUAL, AND THE EROTIC (OUR WORKSHOP EROTIC WEALTH TEACHES YOU HOW TO USE SEX MAGIC AND THE UNCONSCIOUS TO QUANTUM LEAP INTO YOUR NEXT WEALTH EPOCH, ALSO INCLUDED IN YOUR SAFEHOUSE SUBSCRIPTION).

So that's how we ended up here.

five things I wish I knew about launching when I started:

1. There are many, many, many types of launch strategies. Do not get stuck in one. They ALL say they're the best.
That doesn't matter. The best for YOU is all that matters.

2. Your customers love a launch. Don't be afraid of annoying them BUT ALSO

3. Never put your customers through something you do not personally enjoy. Hate automated emails? Don't send them.

4. There is a way to look up exactly what your correct marketing strategy should be. It's in this book.

5. It's 50% mental, 50% hard work. 50% of writing this book was showing up at 2am to put fingers to keyboard. The other 50% was living my life, collecting the information to write about, and being shown the pieces no one could teach me. Skip the hard work, you won't get any results. Skip the magic, you won't get any results.

I WILL LET MY CURRENT LAUNCH STRATEGY SHOW YOU HOW I'M DOING IT NOW, INSTEAD OF EXPLAINING. WHAT I CAN TELL YOU IS THAT I USED TO HATE LAUNCHING AND NOW I LOVE IT. I USED TO STRUGGLE TO MARKET MY WORKSHOPS, NOW I DON'T EVEN THINK ABOUT IT.

I USED TO GET STRESSED, NOW I JUST SHOW UP WHEN I'M STOKED TO SHOW UP. THE MOST I EVER DID PASSIVE INCOME WISE BEFORE THIS WAS 20K. WE'VE DONE 50K, 40K, AND 35K RESPECTIVELY IN THE THREE SLOWEST MONTHS OF THE YEAR THIS YEAR. ALL RECURRING INCOME. NO 1:1.

I SPENT AN ENTIRE YEAR HIRING EXPERTS, USING STRATEGIES, AND CALCULATING IF MY "INSPIRED" , ALIGNED, BUSINESS FLOW ACTUALLY MADE SENSE AND COULD BE TRUSTED. I RIPPED APART EVERY CORNER OF MY BUSINESS THAT HAD SUCCEEDED ACCIDENTALLY, AUDITED IT, AND TOSSED WHATEVER DIDN'T WORK. I MADE 365 DAY CONTENT CALENDARS, TOOK OVER 100 HOURS OF MASTERCLASSES IN EVERYTHING FROM FACEBOOK AND YOUTUBE ADVERTISING TO PR, MARKETING, BESTSELLER WRITING COURSES, SPEAKING COURSES, AND MORE. **THE BOTTOM LINE WAS THIS:**

Anything I did to my design could stay, anything I did out of design had to go. Anything I did that was in my design succeeded, and every time I went out of design I totally and completely fell flat.

Anywhere I worked out of alignment, it cost me and my business months of work with zero profits. Anywhere I worked in alignment, money flew at me so fast it was shocking. Giggle-worthy. WTF-worthy.

Anywhere I was being honest and authentic, it could scale. Anywhere I was lying or faking successful had to go. This included not only my marketing, but my tax filing status, newsletter structure, and even my workout routine.

You can see my tax filing meetings with my accountant in the bonuses on Empress. It's VERY good! I highly recommend. Also included in your Safehouse subscription

So now, we're going to do this for you.

—

I'D LIKE YOU TO **SET AN INTENTION RIGHT NOW, AND GO WRITE IT THREE TIMES IN OUR FUCKLESS CHAT. THIS ROOM IS FILLED WITH YOUR NEW BEST FRIENDS. THE FIRST PEOPLE IN THE WORLD THAT SEE THE "REAL YOU" THAT YOU'VE BEEN TOO SCARED TO SHOW ANYONE ELSE. THESE PEOPLE, THAT YOU HAVEN'T MET YET, ARE GOING TO SHOW YOU HOW OKAY IT IS TO BE YOURSELF.**

YOUR INTERACTION WITH THESE PEOPLE, JUST LIKE YOU, ARE GOING TO BE YOUR REFERENCE POINTS FOR HOW WELL IT WORKS WHEN YOU DO YOU AND STOP FAKING IT FOR APPROVAL. EVERYONE IS MEETING ON THE SAME LEVEL HERE.

DOWNLOAD SAFEHOUSE GLOBAL IN THE APP OR PLAY STORE. GET YOUR FREE VERSION UNDER THE DISCOVER TAB. GO TO THE CHAT, SCROLL TO FUCKLESS, AND DROP YOUR INTENTION THREE TIMES. YOU CAN ALSO INTRODUCE YOURSELF IN THE INTRODUCE YOURSELF CHAT, AND IF YOU WOULD LIKE ME TO PERSONALLY PULL SOME HOMEWORK FOR YOU, YOU CAN DO OUR INTAKE WORKSHOP THAT ONLY TAKES FIVE MINUTES IN THE "HOW TO GET STARTED" WORKSHOP. ITS ON THE NEXT TWO PAGES AS WELL.

TO MAKE SURE YOU DON'T LOSE ANY OF THIS WORK, SHARE WITH US WHAT YOU LEARNED SO FAR. EVERY TIME YOU DO THIS, YOU NOT ONLY BECOME A STRONGER TEACHER, BUT YOU ALSO ANCHOR INTO YOUR MIND THE CONCEPTS YOU MOST NEED TO KNOW. IT BECOMES A PART OF YOUR WISDOM, INSTEAD OF GOING INTO THE KNOWLEDGE SOUP IN YOUR BRAIN WITH EVERY OTHER THING YOU'VE EVER READ, WATCHED, OR LISTENED TO.

COME TELL US IN THE FUCKLESS CHAT ANY A-HA'S YOU HAD HERE! SEE YOU FOR THE NEXT CHAPTER.

MAKE A DOT IN EACH SLICE TO RATE EACH AREA OF LIFE. CENTER REPRESENTS 0/10. EDGE REPRESENTS 10/10. CONNECT THE DOTS TO FORM A CIRCLE AND POST A PICTURE OF THIS PAGE IN #FUCKLESS

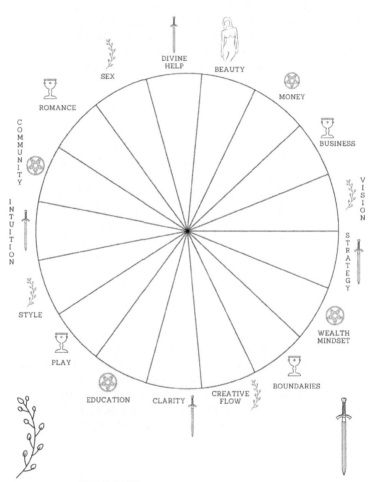

WHAT FOUR AREAS ARE LACKING MOST?

WHAT SPECIFICALLY WOULD YOU LIKE TO
ACHIEVE IN THIS WORKSHOP?

WHAT SPECIFICALLY RESULTS WOULD MAKE THIS THE
10/10, BEST EXPERIENCE EVER FOR YOU?

POST YOUR ANSWER IN #FUCKLESS SO WE CAN GET YOU YOUR
SPECIFIC RECOMMENDATIONS

know yourself, know your market

Positioning
Customer Avatar
Purpose
HD types + strategy
HD Marketing Styles

The equation for authenticity is:

you have to
1. know yourself well enough to
2. trust yourself well enough to
3. be yourself, and know that's
   enough. Both in relationships,
   and in the marketplace.

THE FIRST OF THE THREE PILLARS IN EACH CATEGORY, AUTHENTICITY AND AUTHENTIC MARKETING, IS TO **KNOW**. KNOWING YOURSELF, KNOWING YOUR CUSTOMER, KNOWING YOUR GOAL AND KNOWING YOUR MARKET. THESE THREE WORK SYNERGISTICALLY TO POSITION YOU PERFECTLY FOR YOUR CUSTOMER.

KNOWING YOUR CUSTOMER INVOLVES KNOWING YOURSELF, BECAUSE IN AN ALIGNED BUSINESS, YOUR CUSTOMER IS A REFLECTION OF YOU. A DEEP REFLECTION OF YOU.

WE WILL GO DEEPER INTO WHAT IT MEANS TO TRULY KNOW YOURSELF IN THE FIRST MODULE OF FUCKLESS, WHICH YOU DO HAVE ACCESS TO WHEN YOU DO A FIVE DAY FREE TRIAL OF FUCKLESS ON YOUR SAFEHOUSE GLOBAL APP, SO FOR TODAY WE'RE GOING TO GO INTO YOUR VALUE, AND KNOWING THAT VALUE.

SARA BLAKELY'S CUSTOMERS AT SPANX REFLECTED HER DESIRE TO LOOK SMOOTH AND SLIM IN WHITE PANTS.

THE KEITH FAMILY'S CUSTOMERS FOR THE PERFECT BAR REFLECT THEIR CUSTOMERS' LOVE FOR A QUICK, NUTRITIOUS MEAL REPLACEMENT THAT TASTES GREAT AND PACKS A WALLOP.

MY CUSTOMERS REFLECT MY LOVE FOR THE PERFECT BALANCE OF BUSINESS AND SPIRITUALITY. AN OBSESSION WITH KNOWING THE EXACT RATIOS OF HARD WORK AND MAGIC REQUIRED FOR SUPERNATURAL SUCCESS.

To know your customer is to know yourself.

SO LET'S BEGIN WITH WHAT YOU DO, AND WHY YOU'RE HERE. MOST OF YOU ARE EXPERIENCED IN BUSINESS, BUT IT'S ALWAYS GOOD TO RETURN TO THE ROOTS AND REMEMBER WHY YOU'RE DOING ALL THIS IN THE FIRST PLACE. THESE QUESTIONS GET YOU THERE.

finding your purpose:

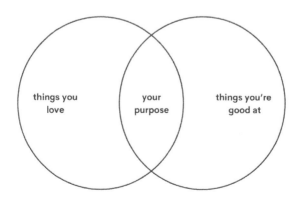

things you love

your purpose

things you're good at

"Trust that the gifts you have are exactly what the world needs. " - Marc Holzman

- WHAT IS THE "LIFEBLOOD" OF YOUR BUSINESS? (YOUR FIRST REACTION IS PROBABLY THE RIGHT ONE)*

- WHAT IS THE BIGGEST COMPETITIVE ADVANTAGE YOU WOULD LIKE TO HAVE?

- WHAT UNFAIR ADVANTAGE DO YOU HAVE IN YOUR INDUSTRY?

- WHAT IS THE THING YOUR CUSTOMERS VALUE THE MOST?

- WHAT IS SOMETHING YOUR COMPETITORS DON'T DO WELL?

- WHAT IS ONE THING YOU DO THAT SEEMS TO MAKE EVERYTHING ELSE EASIER?

- WHAT IS SOMETHING THAT, IF YOU FOCUSED RELENTLESSLY ON IT FOR 5 YEARS, YOU COULD BE WORLD-CLASS AT?

- WHAT DO YOU UNIQUELY BRING?

- WHAT UNIQUE PROBLEMS HAVE YOU SOLVED?

Now, let's learn about your customer avatar:

STEP 1: WRITE OUT AS MUCH INFORMATION AS YOU CAN ABOUT YOUR IDEAL CUSTOMER.

● GIVE THEM A NAME

○ WHERE DO THEY LIVE

○ AGE

● MARRIED OR NOT

● CHILDREN OR NOT

● EDUCATION LEVEL

● JOB FIELD OR PROFESSION

○ JOB TITLE

○ INCOME LEVEL

let's ALWAYS go deeper

STEP 2: WRITE OUT AS MUCH ABOUT THEIR PERSONAL DETAILS AS POSSIBLE.

○ TIME ON JOB

○ SALARY

○ # OF JOBS HELD

○ POLITICAL VIEWS

○ RELIGIOUS VIEWS

○ PERSONAL INTERESTS

○ HOBBIES

STEP 3: WRITE AS MUCH AS POSSIBLE ABOUT THEIR TYPICAL DAY.

● WEBSITES THEY FREQUENT

● BRANDS THEY LOVE

● WHERE THEY GET THEIR NEWS

● INDUSTRY NEWS PUBLICATIONS

● WHAT SOCIAL MEDIA SITES THEY LIKE FROM MOST FAVORITE TO LEAST FAVORITE

● WHAT PERSONAL GOALS DO THEY HAVE

● WHAT BUSINESS GOALS DO THEY HAVE

● WHAT FAMILY GOALS DO THEY HAVE

STEP 4: LIST AT LEAST 3 PROBLEMS THEY HAVE RIGHT NOW THAT YOUR BUSINESS SOLVES.

1. PROBLEM 1

2. PROBLEM 2

3. PROBLEM 3

Now it's time to clarify your goal:

This question is probably the most important question for all spiritual entrepreneurs. Please notice if you have major resistance to answering this, but do not let yourself skip it!

WHAT'S YOUR FINANCIAL GOAL THIS MONTH?

WHAT'S FOR SALE?

HOW MANY NEED TO BE SOLD TO REACH THAT GOAL?

IF YOU HAVE ANY RESISTANCE ANSWERING THIS, OR ANY DIFFICULTY FILLING SOMETHING IN HERE, THEN A WORKSHOP ON MARKETING MIGHT BE A LITTLE ADVANCED FOR YOU. YOU NEED SOMETHING TO MARKET. THE GOOD NEWS IS THAT YOU CAN TOTALLY TAKE THIS AT THE SAME TIME AS ONE OF MY OTHER WORKSHOPS. BOTH BREAKING BROKE 2.0, AND HOW TO START A BUSINESS FROM SCRATCH WILL GET YOU THERE, AND THEY'RE INCLUDED IN THE MONTHLY SUBSCRIPTION JUST LIKE EVERYTHING ELSE.

positioning:

POSITIONING IS ESSENTIAL IN BUSINESS. IF SOMETHING ISN'T POSITIONED CORRECTLY WITHIN THE MARKET, IT CAN'T SELL.

TAKE SARA BLAKELY, FOUNDER OF SPANX FOR EXAMPLE.

WHEN SPANX FIRST GOT PICKED UP BY NEIMAN MARCUS, THEY POSITIONED SPANX IN WITH THE REST OF THE PANTYHOSE, IN THE HOSIERY AISLE. IMAGINE THE PANTYHOSE AISLE IN ANY STORE, WITH ROWS AND ROWS OF DIFFERENT BRANDS OF THE SAME THING. SHE HAD WORKED HARD TO MAKE THE PACKAGING STAND OUT, USING RED, BLACK, AND BOLD ANIMATIONS. STILL, THE PRODUCT WOULDN'T MOVE. SHE HAD CALLED ALL OF HER FRIENDS AND BEGGED THEM TO GO BUY SPANX IN THEIR LOCAL NEIMAN, BUT STILL, THINGS WEREN'T MOVING. SHE WENT TO NEIMAN MARCUS AND NOTICED THAT THE HOSIERY AISLE WAS LOCATED IN SOME FORGOTTEN AREA OF THE STORE. AN AREA THAT PEOPLE DIDN'T BROWSE. THEY WENT FOR SOMETHING SPECIFIC, ONE PAIR, IN AND OUT.

SHE KNEW HER CUSTOMER, FIRST OF ALL. SHE KNEW THAT HER IDEAL CUSTOMER FOR SLIMMING SHAPEWEAR WASN'T IN THE HOSIERY AISLE. THEY WERE IN THE READY-TO-WEAR SECTION. THEY WERE BUYING AN OUTFIT THEY WANTED TO LOOK FABULOUS IN, NOT TIGHTS TO WEAR WITH AN EXISTING OUTFIT. HER CUSTOMERS WERE NOT IN THE HOSIERY AISLE. THEY WERE IN THE READY-TO-WEAR, FITTING ROOMS, AND CHECKOUT LINE. SO THAT'S WHERE SHE WENT.

Do you know who your ideal customer is? Do you know where they are?

WE GO SUPER DEEPLY INTO THE CUSTOMER AVATAR IN MODULE FOUR OF FUCKLESS, BUT IT IS NEVER TOO EARLY TO START THINKING ABOUT WHO THEY ARE, WHERE THEY ARE, AND WHAT KIND OF OFFER THEY CANNOT REFUSE.

SO SHE WENT TO TARGET AND BOUGHT STANDS FOR ORGANIZING ENVELOPES. SHE STOCKED THESE WITH SPANX, AND WENT RIGHT INTO NEIMAN MARCUS AND REPOSITIONED HER PRODUCT. SHE PUT IT BY THE FITTING ROOMS, BY THE CASH REGISTER, AND IN THE READY TO WEAR SECTIONS. SHE HAD NO PERMISSION. IF ANYONE WAS LIKE "WHAT ARE YOU DOING?" SHE JUST TOLD THEM SHE DID HAVE PERMISSION, AND THAT WAS THAT. NO ONE QUESTIONED HER WILL.

BECAUSE OF HOW SHE KNEW HERSELF, KNEW HER CUSTOMER, AND KNEW HER MARKET, SHE WAS ABLE TO POSITION HERSELF CORRECTLY AND SUCCEED. SPANX FLEW OFF THE SHELVES, BUT THAT DIDN'T KEEP HER FROM ROAD TRIPPING AROUND TO EVERY LOCATION, PERSONALLY HYPING UP SPANX IN EACH AND EVERY STORE THAT CARRIED IT.

WHEN SHE SOLD THE MAJORITY STAKE OF SPANX TO BLACKSTONE IN 2021, IT WAS VALUED AT $1.2 BILLION. THAT'S 1200 STACKS OF ONE MILLION DOLLARS. ALL BECAUSE OF THE POWER OF POSITIONING.

ANOTHER EXAMPLE OF THIS IS THE COMPANY PERFECT SNACKS, WHICH IS ONE OF MY FAVORITE SUCCESS STORIES. BUD KEITH WAS A DOOR TO DOOR HEALTH FOOD SALESMAN WITH 13 KIDS. AT 57 HE FELL ILL WITH MELANOMA, TO THE POINT WHERE HE COULD NO LONGER WORK. EVERYTHING WAS IN A DEFICIT. THE FAMILY B&B, THE CAR, EVERYTHING. THE KIDS BANDED TOGETHER AND DEVELOPED A PLAN FOR SAVING THE FAMILY. THEY WOULD SELL DAD'S SIGNATURE PROTEIN BAR THAT HE DEVELOPED FOR THE LONG FAMILY ROAD TRIPS. A SIMPLE, DELICIOUS MIX OF PEANUTS, HONEY, AND VARIOUS PROTEIN AND VEGGIE POWDERS.
THE GOOD NEWS? IT WAS SIMPLE AND DELICIOUS. THE BAD NEWS? IT NEEDED TO BE KEPT IN THE REFRIGERATOR.

Limitations create style.

THAT'S ONE OF THE MOST POWERFUL MANTRAS THAT WAS EVER DIVINELY GIVEN TO ME. AND IT'S ESPECIALLY TRUE IN THE CASE OF THE KEITH FAMILY.

THEY SOLD THEIR B&B FOR $100,000 AND SPENT EVERY LAST DOLLAR ON A CANDY WRAPPING MACHINE AND INGREDIENTS. ONCE THE PRODUCT WAS FINALIZED, THEY FACED SOME SERIOUS POSITIONING ISSUES. AN ENERGY BAR THAT HAS TO BE REFRIGERATED? UNHEARD OF.

BUT, **LIMITATIONS CREATE STYLE.**

SURE, THE FOUNDER HAD TO LIVE IN HIS CAR FOR A MONTH WHILE WAITING FOR THE BAR TO BE PICKED UP BY WHOLE FOODS, BUT ONCE IT WAS, THEY HAD A UNIQUE POSITIONING ADVANTAGE.

THE ENERGY BAR AISLE WAS JAM PACKED AND OVERSTUFFED WITH THE COMPETITION. LUNA BARS, LARA BARS, KIND BARS, AND CLIFF BARS, TO NAME A FEW. LIKE THE HOSIERY AISLE, ENERGY BARS LIVED IN THE WEIRD AISLE WITH ROOM TEMP BULK SODAS AND DIAPERS. BUT IN THE REFRIGERATED SECTION, NEXT TO THE EGGS (A STAPLE FOOD FOR THE MAJORITY OF AMERICANS), THE PERFECT BAR STOOD OUT. THERE WAS NO COMPETITION IN THAT AISLE. IT BECAME THE COMPANY SLOGAN: "THE ORIGINAL REFRIGERATED PROTEIN BAR". **LIMITATIONS CREATE STYLE**, AND BRAND POSITIONING.

Positioning is one of the most crucial aspects of knowing your market, because it's how you demonstrate your relevancy to the customer. If you don't know who you're marketing to, you can't be relevant to them.

If you're not relevant to them, you're annoying them. Like a man getting ads for Diva Cups or a woman getting ads for Viagra.

how does your customer contextualize you? Yes, you are extremely useful, but in what context?

IF SPANX SAYS "WE'RE THE BEST PANTYHOSE" THERE'S NO CONTEXT. IT'S ALL PANTYHOSE. BUT IF SPANX SAYS "WE ARE THE BEST PANTYHOSE FOR SMOOTHING AND SLIMMING THE LOWER BODY" THAT'S THE CONTEXT. THAT'S POSITIONING. IF THAT UNIQUE FORM OF PANTYHOSE IS POSITIONED OUTSIDE THE USUAL PANTYHOSE AISLE, IT'S A RECIPE FOR BILLION-DOLLAR SUCCESS.

NOWADAYS WE HEAR BIG NUMBERS ALL THE TIME, SO HERE'S CONTEXT FOR YOU.

One million seconds is twelve days. One billion seconds is 32 years. A billion is a lot.

TO MAKE IT EVEN MORE CURRENT. SKIMS DID A VERY COMMON POSITIONING TRICK WHERE YOU CAPITALIZE ON SOMEONE ELSE'S RELEVANCY. FOR EXAMPLE IF YOU SELL AN ALL NATURAL SODA AND POSITION IT AS "LIKE COKE, BUT WITH WAY LESS SUGAR.", YOU'RE TAPPING ON THE REAL ESTATE THAT COKE HAS WORKED TO BUILD IN EVERYONE'S MIND, AND THEN VEERING THE AUDIENCE TO YOU. YOU'RE TAKING COKE'S POSITIONING, AND DIVERTING IT TO YOU THROUGH A HIGHLY-RELEVANT-TO-YOUR-CUSTOMER INROAD.

SO WHAT SKIMS DID (AMONG OTHER THINGS) IS SAY "LIKE SPANX, BUT DOESN'T FLATTEN YOUR BUTT.". THERE ARE LAWS NOWADAYS THAT PREVENT YOU FROM CALLING COKE AND SPANX BY NAME, YOU SAY "COLA" AND "SHAPEWEAR" OR "THE LEADING BRAND" BUT PEOPLE KNOW WHAT YOU'RE TALKING ABOUT. WHEN KIM ESSENTIALLY SAID "I LOVED MY SHAPEWEAR, BUT I WOULD ALWAYS HAVE TO CUT THE BUTT BECAUSE THE FLAT-BUTT LOOK IS ONLY APPEALING TO WHITE LADIES IN THE EARLY AUGHTS" , SHE CAPITALIZED ON ALL THE MENTAL REAL ESTATE SPANX HAD WORKED TO CREATE, AND SHIFTED IT HER WAY. SKIMS IS CURRENTLY WORTH $3.2 BILLION. THERE'S NOTHING WRONG WITH DOING THIS. SOMEONE WHO WANTS A FLATTER BUTT WILL PREFER SPANX, AND SOMEONE WHO WANTS REGULAR COKE KNOWS NOTHING TASTES LIKE IT, PERIOD.

So, what makes you RELEVANT to your customer? What makes you stand out? What makes you different?
This is your bio. This is your elevator speech. It's constantly being refined, constantly being re-worked, and since we live in the era of link in bios, there needs to be enough space to also disclose what you're currently marketing. Keep it short.

"I help _____ to _____."
"I teach _____ how to _____."

WHAT'S THE PROBLEM FOR YOUR CUSTOMER?

WHAT'S THE SOLUTION?

WHY ARE YOU THE BEST?

Human Design: Lesson One

Chart, Type,Strategy, Marketing Strategy

THIS IS YOUR HUMAN DESIGN COLORING BOOK, WHICH WILL COME IN VERY HANDY FOR YOU.

I GOT THE IDEA FROM THIS FROM MY FIRST YOGA TEACHER TRAINING, WHERE WE LEARNED ANATOMY VIA THE ANATOMY COLORING BOOK.

IT WAS TEDIOUS AF MEMORIZING THE MUSCLES, BUT ONCE I HAD COLORED IN THE CROSS SECTIONS I ALWAYS REMEMBERED EXACTLY WHAT MUSCLE WAS WHERE, AND WHAT IT'S DEAL WAS.

MY BIGGEST MEH WITH HUMAN DESIGN IS THAT YOU CAN TAKE IN SO MUCH INFORMATION ON YOURSELF IN SUCH A SHORT AMOUNT OF TIME, AND COMPLETELY FORGET TO USE IT. ALSO, YOU'RE TAKING IN SOMEONE ELSE'S INFORMATION ABOUT YOURSELF, SO SOME OF THE MOST USEFUL PIECES OF INFORMATION SIT IN THE KNOWLEDGE DATABASE ALONG WITH RANDOM BUZZFEED ARTICLES AND WIKI HOLES, THAT WILL MAYBE GET DUSTED OFF A FEW YEARS FROM NOW.

I DON'T WANT THAT FOR YOU. I WANT EVERY PIECE OF HUMAN DESIGN THAT YOU GET TO BECOME INSTANT WISDOM FOR YOU.

I WANT YOU TO KNOW EXACTLY WHAT WE'RE TALKING ABOUT, WHERE WE'RE GETTING THE INFORMATION FROM, AND WHAT IT MEANS TO YOU EACH AND EVERY STEP OF THE WAY.

DON'T FILL IN THE HUMAN DESIGN STUFF JUST YET. WE'RE GOING TO BE DOING IT PIECE BY PIECE, AND ONLY FILLING IN A NEW SECTION WHEN WE UNDERSTAND WHAT IT MEANS TO US.

THESE PAGES ARE YOUR BABY! TAKE CARE OF THE BABY!

TYPE:

PROFILE:

DEFINITION:

STRATEGY:

INNER AUTHORITY:

NOT-SELF THEME:

INCARNATION CROSS:

DETERMINATION:

TRAJECTORY:

MOTIVATION:

TRANSFERENCE:

CHANNELS:

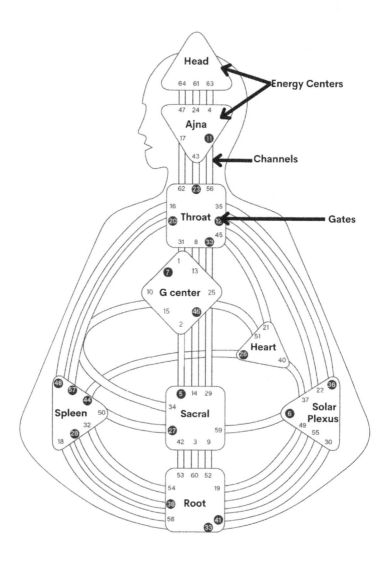

Head

64 61 63

Energy Centers

47 24 4

Ajna

17 **11**

43 ← Channels

62 **23** 56

16 Throat 35

20 **12** ← Gates

31 8 **33** 45

1

7 13

10 G center 25

15 **46**

2

21

51

Heart

26 40

48 57 22 **36**

48 **57** **5** 14 29

44 37 Solar

34 Plexus

Spleen 50 Sacral **6**

27 59 55

32 42 3 9 30

18 **25**

53 60 52

54 19

38 Root

58 **33** **41**

47

unconscious			conscious	
⊙ — —	sun	⊙ — —
⊕ — —	earth	⊕ — —
☽ — —	moon	☽ — —
☊ — —	north node	☊ — —
☋ — —	south node	☋ — —
☿ — —	mercury	☿ — —
♀ — —	venus	♀ — —
♂ — —	mars	♂ — —
♃ — —	jupiter	♃ — —
♄ — —	saturn	♄ — —
⛢ — —	uranus	⛢ — —
♆ — —	neptune	♆ — —
♇ — —	pluto	♇ — —

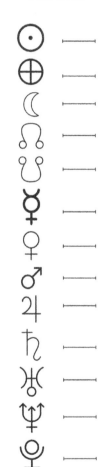

48

HUMAN DESIGN IS A MIX OF ALL WORLD SYSTEMS AND ALL WORLD KNOWLEDGE. BASICALLY A MIX OF ALL THE GREATS, KABBALAH, I CHING, ASTROLOGY, MYERS-BRIGGS, BIOCHEMISTRY, GENETICS, AND THE CHAKRA SYSTEM, TO NAME A FEW.

WE'RE GOING TO START WITH SOMETHING SUPER BASIC HERE, YOUR HUMAN DESIGN TYPE, AND YOUR STRATEGY. I'M SO TEMPTED TO BRING IN YOUR BRAND'S PLANETARY ARRANGEMENT BUT WE HAVE TO GET STRATEGY IN THE MARKETPLACE DONE FIRST, AND YOU NEED TO REMEMBER THAT AF SO...

YOUR STRATEGY IS THE MOST IMPORTANT THING FOR YOU. IT'S THE ONE PIECE OF ADVICE FOR YOUR WHOLE ENTIRE LIFE.

LET'S START BY LOOKING UP YOUR HUMAN DESIGN CHART. YOU CAN ABSOLUTELY GET A FREE ONE, AND IF YOU'RE COMMITTED TO THE FREE OPTION **MYHUMANDESIGN.COM** WILL WORK WELL FOR YOU. IF YOU ARE SERIOUS ABOUT GETTING THE DATA, I RECOMMEND **MAIAMECHANICS.COM**, WHICH IS STRAIGHT FROM THE FOUNDER. IT'S $6 A MONTH. I'VE ALSO USED **GENETICMATRIX.COM**

Q: I DON'T HAVE MY BIRTH DATA, CAN I STILL DO HUMAN DESIGN?

I KNOW A WOMAN WHO WAS GIVEN AWAY AS A CHILD, SO I'M GOING TO WRITE THIS LIKE I'M SPEAKING TO HER.
FIRST OF ALL, I'M SORRY FOR WHATEVER CONDITIONS HAVE MADE IT THAT YOU CAN'T GET YOUR DATA. THAT SUCKS. WHATEVER THE TERMS MAY BE THAT YOU CAN'T GET THIS INFO FROM THE PEOPLE WHO WERE THERE WHEN YOU WERE BORN, THAT SUCKS. IT'S SAD, IT'S FUCKED UP, AND I'M SORRY THAT HAPPENED TO YOU.

HUMAN DESIGN IS SPECIAL IN THE SENSE THAT IT'S EXTREMELY SPECIFIC TO EACH AND EVERY INDIVIDUAL PERSON, AND HAVING AS CORRECT OF A BIRTH TIME AS POSSIBLE IS QUITE IMPORTANT, AND DEFINITELY WORTH HAVING IF YOU'RE INTO ESOTERIC THINGS. IF YOUR PARENTS ARE BALL-PARKING YOUR BIRTHTIME BY 30-60 MINUTES, THE MAIAMECHANICS.COM VERSION HAS A BIRTH TIME RELIABILITY SCORE WHICH WILL HELP YOU LOCATE MAJOR CHANGES IN THE CHART AS A RESULT OF TIME, AND HELP YOU GET A MORE ACCURATE READ.

IN THE US, YOU CAN REQUEST A BIRTH CERTIFICATE FROM VITAL RECORDS WITHOUT YOUR PARENTS, AND SOMETIMES ACCESS ONLINE. IF A QUICK TEXT TO AN ESTRANGED PARENT OR A TRIP TO VITAL RECORDS WEBSITE ISN'T A POSSIBILITY FOR YOU, I UNDERSTAND. THIS COURSE PROBABLY WOULDN'T BE THE MOST FUN WITHOUT THE HUMAN DESIGN, BUT YOU HAVE A NICE LONG PREVIEW OF IT TO DECIDE IF YOU WOULD WANT TO CONTINUE WITHOUT THE HUMAN DESIGN ASPECT OF THIS WORK.

I RECOMMEND THE ENNEAGRAM PERSONALITY TYPES COURSE BY RICHARD ROHR ON YOUTUBE (EIGHT HOURS AND YOU MUST WATCH EVERY SINGLE ONE BEFORE DECIDING WHICH TYPE YOU ARE)IF YOU WANT TO UNDERSTAND A DEEPER PROFESSIONAL VERSION OF YOURSELF, WITH NO BIRTH DATA NECESSARY.

So the very first things we see on our chart are:

- **TYPE:**
- **STRATEGY:**
- **NOT-SELF THEME:**
- **INNER AUTHORITY:**
- **PROFILE:**

THIS IS WHAT WE'LL BE WORKING WITH FIRST.

YOUR TYPE IS WHAT KIND OF ENERGY YOU ARE HERE TO CARRY, AND YOUR RELATIONSHIP TO THAT ENERGY.

YOUR STRATEGY IS HOW TO STAY IN THAT ENERGY.

THE **NOT SELF** THEME IS WHO YOU ARE WHEN YOU ARE OUT OF THAT ENERGY.

THE **INNER AUTHORITY AND PROFILE** WE WILL GET TO LATER ON. ALL YOU NEED TO FOCUS ON RIGHT NOW IS YOUR TYPE.

WE WILL LEARN FIRST, AND THEN RETURN TO THESE PAGES OVER AND OVER AGAIN TO FILL IN.

generators and manifesting generators

IF YOU ARE A GENERATOR, OR MANIFESTING GENERATOR, CONGRATULATIONS! YOU MAKE UP 68% OF THE WORLD. I AM ALSO A GENERATOR, ALONG WITH MY HUSBAND, AND OUR TWO CHILDREN ARE MANIFESTING GENERATORS.

GENERATORS AND MANIFESTING GENERATORS ARE HERE TO BE THE WORKERS OF THE WORLD. WE HAVE CONSISTENT ACCESS TO POWER. WE CAN GO-GO-GO ALL DAY. WE ARE NOT HERE TO HAVE A BEDTIME! IT'S 12:34 AM WHEN I'M WRITING THIS NOW, BECAUSE I AM A GENERATOR AND I CAN WRITE WHENEVER I HAVE THE ENERGY TO DO SO.

GENERATORS, AND MANIFESTING GENERATORS DON'T "GO TO SLEEP". WE PASS OUT. BEDTIME ROUTINES ARE NOT NECESSARY FOR THE GENERATOR CHILD. THEY WILL FALL ASLEEP WHEN THEY'RE TIRED. YOUR GENNY BABY NOT SLEEPING? REMOVE THE NAP! DOES THAT WORK?

MANIFESTING GENERATORS HAVE THE SAME STRATEGY AS THE GENERATORS, AND MOST OF OUR RULES APPLY.

MANIFESTING GENERATORS ARE NOT MANIFESTORS, AT ALL. IT IS NOT THE SAME. DON'T EVEN TRY.

All generators and manifesting generators have sacral authority.

MANIFESTING GENERATORS ARE DIFFERENT FROM GENERATORS IN THE SENSE THAT THEY HAVE THE ABILITY TO MANIFEST, AKA MAKE THINGS HAPPEN WITHOUT GETTING PERMISSION FROM EVERY ALIGNED PLANET, PROVIDING THEY USE THEIR STRATEGY, WHICH WE'LL GET TO IN A MOMENT. USING THEIR STRATEGY IS HARDER FOR THEM, BECAUSE THEY HAVE THIS MOTOR THAT KNOWS THINGS COULD BE DONE FASTER AND BETTER, AND SOMETIMES IT JUST WANTS TO POWER THROUGH. MANIFESTING GENERATORS HAVE CONSISTENT ACCESS TO POWER, SO THEY CAN. **MANIFESTING GENERATORS ARE ALSO MUCH MORE LIKELY TO BE JACK OF ALL TRADES STYLE, WHERE THE GENERATOR CAN PICK ONE THING AND STICK TO IT, AS LONG AS THEY'RE EXCITED ABOUT IT.**

IF YOU ARE A GENERATOR OR A MANIFESTING GENERATOR, CELEBRATE THAT YOU CAN AND WILL DIY. YOU DON'T NEED TO WAIT FOR ANYONE'S PERMISSION. YOU WILL GET IT DONE. YOU WILL MAKE THE CONNECTIONS. YOU WILL BE YOUR AGENT. YOU CAN DO IT ALL, ANYTIME, ANY PLACE. YES, REST IS STILL IMPORTANT, BUT YOU CAN TRUST YOUR DRIVE AND JUST UNDERSTAND THAT THE **REST OF THE HUMAN DESIGN TYPES ARE SO JEALOUS OF TH**E FACT THAT YOU CAN GO AT ANY TIME, ANY PLACE, UNTIL YOU PASS OUT. "DON'T STOP TIL' YOU DROP" IS GOOD MEDICINE FOR THE GENERATOR AND MANI GEN. NOT FOR ANYONE ELSE. FALL IN LOVE WITH THE DIY. YOU WILL MASTER DELEGATING AS YOU GROW. IN THE BEGINNING, STUDY AND BUILD ON REPEAT.

TO AVOID BURNOUT, AND WORKING YOUR BUTT OFF ON A PROJECT THAT WILL GET SCRAPPED, **A GENERATOR WANTS TO MAKE SURE THAT WHAT THEY'RE DOING IS WHAT THEY'RE EXCITED ABOUT.** SINCE A GENERATOR WILL PROBABLY BUILD THEIR OWN WEBSITE, TAKE THEIR OWN PHOTOS, AND WRITE THEIR OWN COPY, WE'LL USE THAT AS A REFERENCE. **ANYTHING YOU'RE INSPIRED ABOUT IS THE BEST THING YOU CAN BE DOING.** TRUST THAT IF YOU DON'T FORCE PHOTOS ON A DAY YOU FEEL LIKE STAYING IN SWEATS, THEN IT MIGHT BE A COPYWRITING DAY. DON'T FORCE YOURSELF TO DO THE TASKS YOU AREN'T EXCITED ABOUT, BUT GO TO WORK ON THE TASKS YOU ARE EXCITED ABOUT. DON'T UNDERESTIMATE THE POWER OF GOING OUTSIDE, OR A GOOD CACA SHOW, LIKE GAME OF THRONES, TO GIVE YOUR MIND A NICE REST.

LIKE A BABBLING BROOK, YOU DO NOT NEED TO BE STILL TO BE CRYSTAL CLEAR.

manifestors

MAKE UP LESS THAN 10% OF THE POPULATION, AND THEY HAVE INCONSISTENT ACCESS TO POWER. **WHEN THEY TAP THAT POWER SOURCE THOUGH, OH MY GOD. THEY CAN REALLY GET THE BALL ROLLING.** THEY HAVE HUGE BURSTS OF ENERGY FOLLOWED BY A NEED FOR DEEP, UNDISTURBED, REST. THIS IS NOT A WEAKNESS OF THEIRS. MANIFESTORS ARE NOT HERE TO BE THE WORKERS OF THE WORLD. **THEY ARE HERE TO GIVE US ALL JOBS. TO SAY "THIS SHIT IS BROKEN, THIS IS HOW YOU'RE GOING TO FIX IT. REPORT BACK TO ME WHEN IT'S DONE."**

MANIFESTORS CAN FEEL ASHAMED AND UNPRODUCTIVE WHEN THEY'RE IN REST MODE, AND IT'S **REALLY CRUCIAL FOR A MANIFESTOR TO UNDERSTAND THAT THE BEST WAY TO GET A BURST OF ENERGY IS TO REST WELL.** A MANIFESTOR CAN OUTRUN A GENERATOR BY A LONG SHOT IN A SPRINT, BUT A MANIFESTOR IS NOT HERE TO BE A MARATHON RUNNER. THEY CAN HIRE A GENNY FOR THAT.

MANIFESTORS DO NOT LIKE BEING TOLD WHAT TO DO, BECAUSE THEY ARE HERE TO TELL OTHER PEOPLE WHAT TO DO. MANIFESTORS HAVE A STRONG ENERGY THAT CAN BE FELT ACROSS THE ROOM. NOT EVERYONE CAN HANDLE THE MANIFESTOR ENERGY, AND THAT'S NOT YOUR PROBLEM.

IF YOU'RE A MANIFESTOR, **I WANT YOU TO UNDERSTAND ON A DEEP LEVEL THAT YOU ARE HERE TO BE YOUR DAMN SELF, AND NOT NEGOTIATE WITH THE REST OF US**. WE CANNOT SURVIVE WITHOUT YOUR DIRECTION. WE NEED YOU TO LAY DOWN THE LAW. WE NEED YOU TO NOT TEXT US WHEN YOU'RE NOT IN THE MOOD. WE NEED YOU TO TAKE YOUR NAPS AND COME BACK WHEN YOU'RE READY. WE NEED YOU TO TELL US HOW IT IS, WHAT THE DEAL IS, AND WHAT DIRECTION WE NEED TO GO IN. A LOT OF US NEVER FEEL READY UNTIL YOU TELL US WE ARE. DON'T FORGET, RA URU HU WAS A MANIFESTOR. HE WASN'T LIKE "HEY HOW DO Y'ALL FEEL ABOUT THIS THING CALLED HUMAN DESIGN?". HE WAS LIKE **"THIS IS WHAT IT IS. YOU DON'T LIKE IT, LEAVE. WE ARE MOVING FORWARD WITH THIS SYSTEM BECAUSE THE WORLD NEEDS IT. THE END."**

ALSO, I KNOW THAT YOU GET ANNOYED WITH HAVING TO INFORM PEOPLE, **BUT WHEN PEOPLE SERVE YOU THE ATTITUDE YOU DIDN'T ORDER, IT'S BECAUSE YOU DIDN'T INFORM THEM SUFFICIENTLY**. ALL THAT SUSPICION, EVEN HOSTILITY, AND REJECTION FROM PEOPLE IS BECAUSE THEY DON'T FEEL INFORMED IN REGARDS TO THIS MASSIVE, NEW DIRECTION THEY KNOW THEY NEED TO GO IN. YOU NEED TO GET COOL WITH INFORMING PEOPLE. THAT'S WHAT YOU ARE HERE TO DO. INFORM PEOPLE UNTIL THEY HAVE NO MORE QUESTIONS. THE QUESTIONS WILL END, AND THEN YOU HAVE THEM FOR LIFE.

IT IS NEVER INCONVENIENT TO SOLVE A PROBLEM

projectors

PROJECTORS ARE THE MOST RECENT ADDITION TO THE HUMAN RACE, THEY'VE BEEN HERE SINCE ABOUT 1782, AND THEY ARE **HERE TO GUIDE THE ENERGY THE GENERATORS CREATE**, AS WELL AS GUIDE THE MANIFESTORS INTO HOW TO USE THEIR ENERGETIC BURSTS MOST EFFECTIVE.

PROJECTORS DO NOT HAVE CONSISTENT ACCESS TO POWER, AND REST IS VERY IMPORTANT TO THEM. THERE'S A KIND OF DISEMPOWERING NARRATIVE AROUND THE PROJECTORS, THAT THEY'RE LIKE, NEEDY PEOPLE WHO WILL GO TO PIECES IF THEY DON'T REST. THIS IS NOT TRUE WHATSOEVER. THEY'RE JUST **NOT HERE TO HUSTLE, OR GET SWEPT UP IN HUSTLE CULTURE. HUSTLE IS FOR PEOPLE (GENERATORS) WHO MAKE MANY MORE MISTAKES THAN A PROJECTOR, AND NEED THE ADDITIONAL HOURS TO CLEAN UP THE MESS ;)**

There are three different kinds of projectors

MENTAL PROJECTORS, ENERGY PROJECTORS, AND CLASSIC PROJECTORS, AND YOUR CHART WILL TELL YOU WHICH ONE YOU ARE.

MENTAL PROJECTORS: YOU ARE A MENTAL PROJECTOR IF YOU HAVE TWO OR THREE OF THE TOP THREE CENTERS DEFINED BUT NO DEFINITION BELOW THE THROAT. MENTAL PROJECTORS ARE RARE. AS A MENTAL PROJECTOR, YOU'RE HERE TO LEARN FOR LIFE. MENTAL PROJECTORS NEED TO BOUNCE IDEAS OFF OF OTHERS AROUND THEM IN ORDER TO GAIN CLARITY. THIS DOES NOT MEAN TAKING ADVICE, BUT USING OTHERS AS A SOUNDING BOARD TO HELP YOU CONNECT TO YOUR AUTHENTIC FEELINGS ABOUT AN INVITATION. SOCIAL MEDIA IS GREAT FOR THIS.

ENERGY PROJECTORS HAVE AT LEAST ONE CONSISTENT AND RELIABLE SOURCE OF ENERGY, THEY MAY NOT FIT THE CLASSIC PROJECTOR STEREOTYPE OF BEING TIRED OR EASILY BURNED OUT. YOU ARE AN ENERGY PROJECTOR IF YOU HAVE A DEFINED MOTOR CENTER. A MOTOR CENTER IS THE ROOT, SOLAR PLEXUS, OR HEART. DEFINED MEANS IT'S COLORED-IN AND NOT WHITE, AND MEANS THAT YOU SUPPLY YOUR OWN ENERGY THERE, IT'S NOT WHERE YOU'RE OPEN TO BE FILLED IN BY OTHERS. THEREFORE YOU COULD BE AN EMOTIONAL PROJECTOR (FROM THE SOLAR PLEXUS) OR A EGO PROJECTOR FROM THE HEART,

THE CLASSIC PROJECTOR TYPE INCLUDES SPLENIC PROJECTORS (WITH NO CONNECTION TO THE HEART CENTER OR ROOT CENTER) AND SELF-PROJECTED PROJECTORS. THESE ARE THE CLASSIC PROJECTOR ARCHETYPE TYPICALLY PORTRAYED AS BEING EASILY DRAINED OF ENERGY AND THEREFORE REQUIRING LOTS OF REST, CLASSIC PROJECTORS SHOULD TAKE TIME TO EXAMINE WHERE THEY'RE EXPENDING THEIR ENERGY LEVEL. ARE THE INVITATIONS YOU'RE ACCEPTING ONES THAT TRULY LIGHT YOU UP AND ALIGN WITH YOUR ENERGY?

NOTE: YOUR SACRAL CENTER WILL ALWAYS BE OPEN BECAUSE OTHERWISE YOU'D BE A GENERATOR RATHER THAN A PROJECTOR, BUT ANY OF YOUR OTHER THREE MOTOR CENTERS (SOLAR PLEXUS (EMOTIONAL), THE EGO (HEART) CENTER, OR THE ROOT CENTER) MAY BE DEFINED.

BECAUSE **NO PROJECTORS HAVE SACRAL AUTHORITY**, IT'S IMPORTANT TO NOTE THAT IF THEY'RE SURROUNDED BY GENERATORS THEY CAN GET REVVED UP ON THAT ENERGY THE GENERATORS PROVIDE, AND CONFUSE IT WITH THEIR OWN. ONCE THE GENERATORS LEAVE THE BUILDING, THE PROJECTORS REALIZE "OH SHIT, I'M FUCKING TIRED.". IF THAT HAPPENS AS A LIFESTYLE, THE PROJECTOR IS GOING TO GET EXHAUSTED WHICH LEADS TO THE PROJECTOR GETTING ILL.

reflectors

REFLECTORS ARE THE RARE BIRDS, THEY MAKE UP JUST 1% OF THE POPULATION BUT SHIT IF A LOT OF THAT 1% DOESN'T FIND ME! **MY FIRST PIECE OF ADVICE FOR A REFLECTOR IS DO NOT COMPARE YOURSELF TO ANYBODY.** IT'S A LOSING GAME. AND YOU ARE NOT UNPRODUCTIVE, OR NOT DOING "ENOUGH". YOU DO THINGS ON REFLECTOR TIME. FULL STOP. **COMPARE YOURSELF TO THE MOON**. A PHASE FOR EVERYTHING. THINGS GET DONE ON A MONTH BY MONTH BASIS, AND NO ONE THAT ISN'T A REFLECTOR REALLY UNDERSTANDS WHAT IT'S LIKE TO BE YOU. IF YOU'RE GOING TO HIRE A COACH, HIRE A REFLECTOR WHO CAN PLAY YOUR GAME, AND THAT YOU LOOK UP TO IN YOUR FIELD. BE CONSCIOUS ABOUT HIRING A GENERATOR MENTOR BECAUSE YOU THINK YOU WILL GET GENERATOR BEHAVIOR BY BEING AROUND THEM ALL THE TIME. YOU WILL, FOR A MINUTE, BUT IT'S UNSUSTAINABLE AND WILL WEAR OFF THE SECOND YOU LEAVE THE BUILDING.

A REFLECTOR IS A DIFFERENT PERSON EVERY DAY. YOU CAN ONLY REALLY UNDERSTAND THEM WHEN YOU'VE WATCHED THEM FOR SEVERAL LUNAR CYCLES AND SEE THEIR UNIQUE PATTERNING START TO ARISE.

A REFLECTOR'S CHART IS COMPLETELY OPEN. NO CENTERS DEFINED, EVERY CENTER WHITE. THIS MEANS THAT THEY ARE OPEN TO EVERYTHING AND ATTACHED TO NOTHING. THEY ARE HERE TO FILTER THE WORLD BY TAKING IT ALL IN, AND OVER THE COURSE OF A LUNAR CYCLE, PICKING AND CHOOSING WHAT'S A FIT FOR THEM.

IT'S A REALLY UNIQUE PROCESS AND OF ALL THE HUMAN DESIGN TYPES, I'M THE MOST ADAMANT THAT WHEN IT COMES TO REFLECTORS IN BUSINESS, THAT THEY SHOULD ONLY GET 1:1 MENTORED BY OTHER REFLECTORS WHEN IT COMES TO BUSINESS COACHING. FOR SPIRITUAL TEACHING, HIRE ANYONE, BUT FOR PRODUCTIVITY - REFLECTORS ONLY. THEY GET IT, AND ACCEPTING THE REFLECTOR NATURE IS A HARD THING TO GET. SO, FOR EXAMPLE, WE'LL PUT A 40 DAY CHALLENGE IN THE WORK ONCE YOU HAVE YOUR MESSAGING CLEAR. A REFLECTOR WILL PROBABLY NEED TO TAKE A MONTH TO SEE IF THAT WORKS FOR THEM.

REFLECTORS AREN'T CLEAR UNLESS THEY WAIT A LUNAR CYCLE. EVERYTHING WILL SEEM LIKE A DECENT OR TERRIBLE IDEA UNTIL IT'S CRYSTAL CLEAR WHAT DIRECTION THEY SHOULD BE GOING IN, WHICH ONLY OCCURS AFTER A FULL LUNAR CYCLE. WHEN IT'S MURKY FOR THE REFLECTOR, ITS MURKY FOR EVERYONE ELSE.

REFLECTORS, I DON'T GIVE A SHIT IF YOU THINK YOUR TIMING IS FAIR OR IF YOU LIKE IT OR NOT. YOU'RE THE 1%. IT IS WHAT IT IS. A LUNAR CYCLE.

REFLECTORS HOLD A MIRROR TO THE WORLD, ASSESS THE BIG PICTURE, AND SAY "WHAT NEEDS TO BE ASSESSED HERE, FOR THE COLLECTIVE?"

We could say that a Manifestor provides the blueprint for the buildings, the Generators are the construction workers, the Manifesting Generators find the shortcuts in the building process, the Projectors act as the foreman, making sure all the workers do their jobs correctly, and the Reflectors go in last to assess the overall safety and functionality of the building itself, as well as its presence in the community. Everyone has a job to do.

HD types as fashion houses

PROJECTORS GIVE CHANEL. THAT MEANS A STATEMENT PIECE. **GENERATORS AND MANIFESTING GENERATORS GIVE BASICS. CALVIN KLEIN**. NOW LOOK. I KNOW SO MANY GENNIES THAT WERE LIKE "FUCK HUMAN DESIGN, IF I'M NOT A UNICORN.". GIRL, STOP. I KNOW UNICORNS, AND THEY'RE FUCKIN' SICK OF BEING A UNICORN.

BASICS ARE WHAT PEOPLE ACTUALLY WEAR EVERY DAY. THE RICHER SOMEONE IS, THE MORE BASIC THEIR WARDROBE LOOKS. IT'S STEALTH WEALTH. MY CALVINS. A NICE WHITE TEE, AND SOME EXCELLENT JEANS. I'M GOING TO ASSUME THE GENERATORS WILL JUST GET OVER IT ME CALLING THEM BASICS (NOT BASIC) BY REMINDING YOU THAT MY WHOLE FAMILY, AND ME, ARE GENNIES AND WE'RE THE MF DREAM TEAM. A FOR ATTITUDE BABY!

BUT DAMN, A STATEMENT PIECE GOES A LONG WAY. THAT ONE PIECE OF PROJECTOR ADVICE CAN ELEVATE THE ENTIRE LOOK AND MAKE IT DINNER READY, AND IT IS NOT SOMETHING THAT YOU HAVE TO BUY A FRESH ONE OF EVERY SIX MONTHS BECAUSE YOU WORE IT INTO THE GROUND. IT'S BUILT TO LAST. YOU'RE NOT GOING TO BE TOO MORTIFIED ABOUT IT IMMEDIATELY AFTER WEARING IT.

I SAY THIS ALL THE TIME TO MY CLIENTS WHO ARE CONCERNED ABOUT MAKING MISTAKES. "THE ONLY WAY YOU CAN LIVE A LIFE WITH NO FASHION REGRETS IS TO START WEARING CHANEL EVERY DAY WHEN YOU'RE TWELVE YEARS OLD. AKA DRESSING LIKE BUNNY MACDOUGAL OR ANY OTHER OLD ASS LADY, EVERY SINGLE DAY IN YOUR YOUTH. THAT'S SOME LILY-ROSE SHIT. IT'S LAME. TAKE RISKS. MAKE MISTAKES.

PROJECTORS, THE CHANEL OF THE WORLD, THEY'RE NOT HERE TO BE EVERY DAY. THEY ARE HERE TO BE THE GUESTS OF HONOR, INVITED FOR THEIR UNIQUE EXPERTISE AND TALENT AND SHOWN OFF.

WE COULD CALL **MANIFESTORS IN THE FASHION WORLD THE YEEZY** (EVEN THOUGH HE'S A SPLENIC PROJECTOR). SOMEONE WHO DEFINITELY UNDERSTANDS WHERE THE TRENDS ARE AT AND DOESN'T ASK ANYONE IF THEY THINK THAT RUNNERS SHORTS ARE TOO BASIC, THEY JUST TELL PEOPLE, "THIS IS WHERE WE ARE GOING."

WE ALL KNOW ABOUT HOW YE'S CAREER SPIRALED OUT WHEN HE REFUSED TO INFORM PEOPLE WHAT THE ARTISTIC VISION WAS BEHIND HIS "WHITE LIVES MATTER" SHIRT. PEOPLE GOT SUSPICIOUS AND ANGRY, AND HE REFUSED TO INFORM THEM AS TO WHAT HIS ARTISTIC STATEMENT WAS, WHICH RESULTED IN ONE BIG ANGRY DOWNWARD SPIRAL. NO ONE CAN DENY THE MAN'S GENIUS, BUT HIS FAILURE TO INFORM RESULTED IN OSTRACIZATION, EXILE, BURNED BRIDGES, AND OTHER INCONVENIENCES. I GUESS WE WILL SEE IF IT LASTS! I BELIEVE IN YE'S TALENT! AND WHEN WE BREAK DOWN SOME PEOPLE'S CHARTS LATER IN THE BOOK, HIS WILL BE ONE OF THEM.

REFLECTORS REALLY REPRESENT JEWELRY. IT'S NOT CLOTHES, BUT IT'S NOT A REAL OUTFIT WITHOUT JEWELRY. WHEN PEOPLE ARE WONDERING WHY THEIR WHITE T-SHIRT AND JEANS DOESN'T HAVE THAT POLISHED LOOK, IT'S BECAUSE OF THE JEWELRY. IT CAN BE A FORGOTTEN ASPECT, WHICH DRIVES THE REFLECTORS CRAZY, BUT ONCE YOU NOTICE IT YOU CANNOT LIVE WITHOUT IT. JEWELRY IS FOR THE COLLECTIVE. THERE ARE SO MANY DIFFERENT STYLES, SO MANY METALS, SO MANY KINDS OF JEWELRY LIKE RINGS AND BRACELETS, BUT IT REALLY IS FOR EVERYONE. THERE'S NO ONE THAT DOESN'T APPRECIATE ANY KIND OF JEWELRY. IF IT'S NOT FOR THEM, AT LEAST THEY LIKE IT ON OTHERS.

Let's go fill in the most essential part of your human design chart, your TYPE, which we just learned. Do that, then come back here.

You can trust me on this Human Design tip when I say, you do not need to understand the whole chart today. It is so much better to take in one piece at a time and really understand what that means for you, and remember it, than to flood yourself with information and not remember any of it. This is the chief limitation I find with people and human design. In one ear, out the other. Now answer in our Fuckless chat on the app or here :

What does being a _ _ _ _ _ _ _ _ _ _ _ _ _ _ _ _ mean to you?
Does it resonate?

your strategy

EACH HUMAN DESIGN TYPE HAS A SPECIFIC FEELING SIGNATURE THAT LETS THEM KNOW OBJECTIVELY WHEN THEY ARE ALIGNED, AND WHEN THEY ARE NOT ALIGNED.

IN HUMAN DESIGN THIS IS CALLED THE **SELF** AND THE **NOT-SELF** THEME.

YOUR STRATEGY IN HUMAN DESIGN IS ONE SOLID RULE FOR LIFE THAT LETS YOU KNOW WHAT YOU CAN DO, ALWAYS AND FOREVER IN LIFE, TO STAY ALIGNED AND NOTICE WHEN YOU ARE OUT OF ALIGNMENT, WHICH IS JUST AS IMPORTANT.

Q: SO WHAT IS A STRATEGY AGAIN?
IT'S YOUR ONE SOLID RULE FOR FINDING OBJECTIVE ALIGNMENT IN YOUR LIFE, OVER AND OVER AGAIN.

Q: SO WHAT IS THE SELF AND NOT-SELF AGAIN?
THE SELF IS WHO YOU ARE WHEN YOU'RE ALIGNED, AND THE NOT-SELF IS WHO YOU ARE WHEN YOU'RE NOT ALIGNED. WE'LL USE THESE TERMS A LOT IN THIS WORK, BECAUSE FUCKLESS IS ALL ABOUT LEARNING AND HARNESSING YOUR INDIVIDUAL EXPRESSION OF ALIGNMENT.

SAY "MOO" IF YOU UNDERSTAND.

for generators and mani gens

THE SELF, OR ALIGNED FEELING SIGNATURE IS *SATISFACTION*. WHEN A GENERATOR OR MANIFESTING GENERATOR IS ALIGNED THEY FEEL **SATISFIED**.

wait to respond

is the strategy for generators and manifesting generators

WHEN A GENERATOR OR MANIFESTING GENERATOR IS NOT ALIGNED, THEY FEEL **FRUSTRATED**. **FRUSTRATION** IS A SIGN THAT A GENERATOR OR A MANIFESTING GENERATOR IS NOT IN ALIGNMENT.

HOW A GENERATOR CAN GET INTO ALIGNMENT AND STAY IN ALIGNMENT IS BY WAITING TO RESPOND. THE STRATEGY OF GENERATORS AND MANIFESTING GENERATORS IS "WAIT TO RESPOND". THE RESULT OF WAITING TO RESPOND IS SATISFACTION. THE RESULT OF NOT WAITING TO RESPOND IS FRUSTRATION.

LIFE WILL ASK GENERATORS: "DO YOU WANT TO DO THIS? DOES THIS SEEM CORRECT TO YOU?" AND OTHER YES/NO QUESTIONS. THE GENERATOR'S JOB IS TO RESPOND TO THESE QUESTIONS THAT LIFE NATURALLY PRESENTS BASED ON IF IT'S A HELL YEAH OR A HELL NO.
WHEN THE GENERATOR STARTS BUILDING SOMETHING OR GOING IN A DIRECTION THAT IS NOT IN RESPONSE TO SOMETHING, OR IN RESPONSE TO SOMETHING THAT IS NOT CORRECT FOR IT, IT'S LIKE TIRES SPINNING IN THE MUD. THERE IS NOTHING TO RESPOND TO, AND THEY FEEL STUCK AND FRUSTRATED.

AN INTERESTING FACT ABOUT GENERATORS IS THAT THEY TELL THEIR TRUTH IN SOUNDS MORE OFTEN THAN WORDS, BECAUSE THEY HAVE THAT LOW-LOW, PRIMAL, SACRAL DEFINITION.
SO IF I ASK MY GENERATOR HUSBAND "DO YOU WANT TO GO EAT BRUNCH?" AND HE SAYS "MEEEEEEEEEHHHHHHHHHH, YEAH." , THE "MEH" IS TELLING THE TRUE ANSWER, THE "YEAH" IS WHAT HE THINKS I WANT TO HEAR. IF I ASK HIM IF HE UNDERSTANDS AND HE GOES "HMMMMMMMMM..... YEAH." THE "HMMMMM" IS THE TRUTH, AND THE YEAH IS WHAT HE THINKS I WANT TO HEAR.
I SUPER RECOMMEND, FOR GENERATORS, TO INVITE PEOPLE TO ANSWER BY MAKING A SOUND.

MANIFESTING GENERATORS CAN USE THEIR WORDS, "YES/NO" , BUT YOU WANT TO SET THEM UP WITH A NICE "YES/NO" QUESTION. FOR EXAMPLE, I WOULDN'T ASK MY SON WHAT HE WANTS TO EAT FOR BREAKFAST. I WOULD ASK "DOES SAUSAGE SOUND GOOD TO YOU?" SO HE CAN SAY YES OR NO.

marketing for
generators and mani gens

GENERATORS ARE THE TALK SHOW HOSTS OF THE WORLD. THE REALITY TV STARS. YOU ARE HERE FOR QUANTITY, AND STAYING ON TOP OF/ RESPONDING TO CURRENT WORLD TRENDS OR WHAT IS CURRENTLY POPPING OFF FOR YOU RIGHT NOW. "WORK WHEN YOU'RE INSPIRED, ON WHATEVER YOU'RE INSPIRED ABOUT RIGHT NOW" IS GOOD MEDICINE FOR ALL HD TYPES, BUT ESPECIALLY FOR OUR GENERATORS AND MANIFESTING GENERATORS.

KIM KARDASHIAN COULD EASILY BEAT HERSELF UP FOR NOT BEING AN ACADEMY AWARD WINNING ACTRESS, BUT SHE'S NOT HERE TO DELIVER THE CHANEL. SHE'S HERE TO DELIVER THE BASICS, AND THAT'S WHY PEOPLE JUST EAT HER ON UP. SHE'S NOT HERE TO BE MYSTERIOUS, OR TO POST ONE STORY A DAY. SHE'S HERE FOR THE VOLUME, AND WE ARE HERE FOR THAT. GIVE US ALL THE STORIES. TELL US A MILLION TIMES. GIVE US A MILLION PRODUCTS.

THE GENERATOR CAN CREATE A WIIIIIIIIIDE PRODUCT RANGE. YOU ARE HERE TO CREATE MANY OF WHATEVER IT IS THAT YOU'RE MAKING BECAUSE YOU'LL BE FUCKING MISERABLE IF YOU'RE TRYING TO JUST SELL ONE THING EVERY DAY.

WHEN YOU HAVE A WIDE PRODUCT RANGE, AND AUTHENTIC MARKETING, YOU CAN TALK TO YOUR AUDIENCE ABOUT WHATEVER, WHENEVER, AND WITH INTENTION, IT WILL FILTER BACK TO ONE OF YOUR PRODUCTS AND BE A SALES FUNNEL FOR THAT.
IT'S ALL ABOUT NOT LETTING YOURSELF GET BORED, AND ALL ABOUT RESPONDING TO WHATEVER IS PEAKING FOR YOU RIGHT NOW.

THE GENERATOR AND MG VIBE IS ALL ABOUT THE **E N E R G Y**, WHICH YOU HAVE ON A DAILY BASIS. GIVE YOURSELF PERMISSION TO BOLDLY PURSUE OR POST ABOUT WHATEVER YOU'RE INSPIRED ABOUT, NO MATTER HOW RANDOM IT SEEMS. IT'S NOT RANDOM, THIS IS WHAT HAS BEEN GIVEN TO YOU TO RESPOND TO. THAT ENERGY IS CONTAGIOUS. IF YOU USE THE ENERGY TO TRY TO FORCE YOURSELF TO WRITE SOMETHING YOU DON'T WANT TO WRITE ABOUT, THERE IS NO ENERGY. THERE'S NO CHILI AND LIME ON THAT SHIT. IT FALLS FLAT.

GENERATORS STRUGGLE AND FEEL LIKE THEY'RE LOSING THEIR WAY WHEN IT FEELS LIKE THERE'S NOTHING TO RESPOND TO, AKA SURRENDER TIME. NO RESPONSE IS A RESPONSE.

WHEN IT SEEMS LIKE THERE'S NOTHING TO DO, STUDY OR GO THE FUCK OUTSIDE AND TALK TO PEOPLE! OR READ SOME TABLOIDS LIKE A TALK SHOW HOST. WHEN IT COMES TO STUDY, IF YOU READ A SPIRITUALITY BOOK LAST, READ A BUSINESS BOOK NEXT AND VICE VERSA. IT'S CRUCIAL TO WORK BOTH ARMS OF LIFE, THE FAITH ARM AND THE WORKS ARM. OR YOU CAN BE ONE OF MY STUDENTS AT SAFEHOUSE. WE ALWAYS WORK BOTH IN EQUAL MEASURE. ANCIENT MAGIC, MODERN BUSINESS.

Q&A IS GREAT FOR GENERATORS, BECAUSE THERE'S SO MUCH TO RESPOND TO. I RECOMMEND INVOLVING Q&A IN YOUR GENERATOR- LED BUSINESS AS MUCH AS POSSIBLE TO REALLY GET A CONVERSATION GOING. ESPECIALLY IF YOU NEED TO CLOSE A CART OR DO SOMETHING TIMELY AND YOU'RE LACKING INSPIRATION, JUST ASK THE AUDIENCE SO YOU CAN HAVE SOMETHING TO RESPOND TO! WHEN WE TALK ABOUT SALES TRIGGERS IN MODULE FOUR AND SIX, YOU'LL LEARN THAT PEOPLE WILL BUY WHATEVER THEY HELP BUILD, SO INVOLVE THEM.

A generator is the Carrie Bradshaw of SATC

ALWAYS RESPONDING TO WHAT HER LIFE HANDED HER IN HER COLUMN.

ON SAFEHOUSE WE HAVE A CHANNEL CALLED MORNING ROUTINE, WHICH IS GREAT FOR EVERYONE BUT ESPECIALLY FOR GENERATORS. IT'S THREE QUESTIONS I START EVERY DAY WITH, THAT I CAN RESPOND TO, TO MAKE SURE I'M ALWAYS IN ALIGNMENT IN THE THREE AREAS OF LIFE. BUSINESS, PLEASURE, AND GOD. THE THREE QUESTIONS ARE:

WHAT DO YOU WANT TO DO TODAY? (NOT "SHOULD" OR "NEED")

IF YOU COULD ONLY GET ONE THING DONE TODAY, WHAT WOULD IT BE?

HOW CAN GOD BLESS YOU TODAY?

TRY IT!

for projectors

THE ALIGNED SELF'S FEELING SIGNATURE IS **SUCCESS**. THE NOT-SELF'S FEELING SITUATION IS **BITTERNESS**.
NOW, THE KEY TO FEELING SUCCESSFUL AND NOT BITTER IS IN THE PROJECTOR'S STRATEGY, WHICH IS WAIT FOR THE INVITATION.

wait for the invitation
is the strategy for projectors

WHEN PROJECTORS WAIT TO BE INVITED, THEIR UNIQUE, LASERED IN PERSPECTIVES ARE WELL RECEIVED. **WHEN THEY DON'T WAIT TO BE INVITED, THEIR PERSPECTIVE IS USUALLY REJECTED.** PEOPLE DON'T VALUE CHANEL THEY DIDN'T PAY FOR. THEY'LL BE LIKE? "PINK TWEED? NO THANKS". THAT **REJECTION MAKES THE PROJECTOR FEEL LIKE SHIT,** WHICH MAKES THEM FEEL BITTER.

FEELING BITTER IS AN AWFUL WAY TO FEEL, AND YOU CAN REALLY NOTICE IT IN A PROJECTOR'S VOICE ON SOCIAL MEDIA. IF A PROJECTOR (OR ANY TYPE) IS REALLY ACTIVE ON SOCIAL MEDIA, THEY'LL FEEL ACTIVE WHEN THEY'RE IN THEIR NOT SELF AS WELL. THERE CAN BE LONG RANTS ABOUT WHAT'S WRONG AND WHO'S WRONG AND WHY IT'S SO FRUSTRATING, AND THE BITTERNESS IS REALLY TANGIBLE. IT'S NOT THAT IT'S "BAD", IT'S JUST NOT DOING ANYTHING TO STRENGTHEN YOUR BRAND. WE'LL TALK ABOUT THE NOT-SELF AS A PORTAL TO CREATION IN A BIT, BUT FOR NOW, WE'RE LOOKING AT BITTERNESS.

PROJECTORS CAN GET SO BITTER WHEN IT FEELS LIKE THERE ARE NO INVITATIONS COMING THEIR WAY, AND A KEY PIECE TO RECOGNIZE IS THAT A PART OF THE PROJECTOR'S JOB IS USING YOUR SKILLS TO BECOME SOMEONE, SOMEWHERE, THAT IS EASILY INVITED.

THIS COULD MEAN BUILDING YOUR SOCIAL MEDIA AUDIENCE WHILE WAITING FOR THE PODCAST INVITE.

THIS COULD MEAN GOING TO THE COFFEE SHOP WITH YOUR TAROT DECK OUT WHILE WAITING FOR PEOPLE TO ASK YOU TO DO A TAROT SPREAD FOR THEM (NOT FOR FREE, OBVIOUSLY).

64

IT COULD MEAN PRACTICING IN THE MIRROR EXACTLY WHAT YOUR RELEVANCY IS, SO THAT WHEN SOMEONE ASKS YOU WHAT YOU DO, WHICH IS AN INVITATION, YOU KNOW EXACTLY WHAT TO SAY TO GET MORE INVITES.

ALSO, FOR THE PROJECTORS, **SPEND YOUR WAITING TIME STUDYING AND PREPARING, STUDYING AND PREPARING. WHEN THE TEACHER IS READY, THE STUDENT APPEARS.** THE INVITATIONS WILL COME, IT'S WHAT YOU WERE MADE FOR.

YOU DO NOT NEED TO SAY YES TO EVERY INVITATION YOU GET, IT'S ABOUT CHOOSING THE ONES THAT FEEL RIGHT ON THE MONEY FOR YOU.

A projector is the Miranda Hobbes of SATC

SHE'S NEVER AFRAID TO TAKE A NIGHT INDOORS, AND IS OFTEN TIMES ALIENATING PEOPLE WHEN SHE DROPS THE **UNINVITED** NEWS ON THEM LIKE "HE'S JUST NOT THAT INTO YOU".

SHE'S IN A **POSITION OF LEADERSHIP IN HER JOB** WHERE SHE'S RECOGNIZED AND INVITED TO WORK ON CERTAIN CASES AND HER INPUT IS VALUED. SHE'S NOT HOLDING A SANDWICH BOARD OUT IN THE STREET SAYING "FREE ADVICE". SHE'S DRESSED LIKE A LAWYER ALL THE TIME, LOOKING THE PART, READY FOR THE INVITE.

marketing for projectors

YOU ARE HERE TO BE CHANEL, AND YOU CAN PROVIDE QUALITY OVER QUANTITY. **DON'T HESITATE TO REALLY LAY THE BUSINESS ON YOUR SOCIAL MEDIA FEED. TO POST ONE VIDEO A WEEK BUT SUPER HIGH QUALITY, POLISHED, AND LOADED WITH SUPER SOLID ADVICE. OR OFF THE CUFF, BUT NOT MINCING ANY WORDS.** PEOPLE CAN CRAVE YOU, BEG FOR YOU, WAIT ALL WEEK FOR YOUR POSTS. YOUTUBE IS A GOOD PLATFORM FOR THIS AS WELL, FYI, BECAUSE THEY DON'T CARE HOW INFREQUENTLY YOU POST, AS LONG AS IT'S THE GOOD SHIT WHEN YOU DO POST. ANY HD TYPE CAN DO ANY PLATFORM, THOUGH. **WHEN IT COMES TO YOUR CONTENT, DON'T HOLD BACK! REALLY, REALLY TEACH US WHAT'S UP. DEVELOP A REPUTATION FOR HAVING INSANELY VALUABLE CONTENT, BASED ON YOUR EXPERIENCE AND UNIQUE PERSPECTIVES.**

PEOPLE COME TO US GENERATORS TO SEE SOMEONE EVERY DAY, BUT **YOU ARE SPECIAL. DON'T GET STUCK IN THE HUSTLE POSTING, AND IGNORE ANY STRATEGY THAT HAS YOU SHOWING UP EVERY DAY**. NO ONE WEARS CHANEL EVERY DAY AND LOOKS GOOD UNLESS THEY'RE 95 YEARS OLD. SAVE IT FOR A SPECIAL INVITE AND TRUST IT'S GETTING THE JOB DONE.

ANOTHER PRO TIP FOR YOU PROJECTORS IN ONLINE BUSINESS IS THAT **YOU GUIDE THE ENERGY THAT OTHERS CREATE**, SO RECOGNIZE THE ASPECT OF YOUR GENIUS THAT CAN SEE EASILY "THERE'S A WHOLE LOT OF THIS GOING ON, BUT NOT A LOT OF THAT". TAP THAT. THAT IS THE INVITATION.

YOU'RE THE OPERATIONS MANAGER, LOCATING THE BOTTLENECKS AND TELLING US EXACTLY WHAT NEEDS TO BE DONE TO MAKE SURE IT DOESN'T HAPPEN AGAIN. GIVE IT TO US STRAIGHT.

THAT'S WHY IT'S SO, SO KEY TO BE AUTHENTIC ON THE INSIDE, AND NOT ATTEMPT TO MARKET AUTHENTICALLY WITHOUT IT. IT'S NOT POSSIBLE. AUTHENTICITY IS KNOWING YOURSELF WELL ENOUGH TO TRUST YOURSELF, AND THEN TRUSTING YOURSELF WELL ENOUGH TO BE YOURSELF AND KNOW THAT THAT IS ENOUGH. FIRST INTERNALLY, THEN IN THE MARKETPLACE.

Assessing the excess, undirected energy in the world and knowing where to guide it IS an online invitation for the projector.

FOR BEST RESULTS, PUT IT ON YOUR FEED, NOT IN SOMEONE ELSE'S COMMENTS.

IN ORDER TO BE RECOGNIZED, YOU HAVE TO SHOWCASE WHAT YOU KNOW. YOU KNOW SO MUCH. IT DOESN'T MATTER WHAT YOUR AGE IS.

FUCKLESS IS GOING TO TEACH YOU MORE AND MORE ABOUT RELAXING AND LETTING YOUR INNER KNOWING SHOW, BUT IN THE MEANTIME, YOU NEED TO **HONOR THAT YOU ARE A GUIDE**. YOU HAVE BEEN THERE AND DONE THAT. IF YOU HAVE NOT BEEN THERE AND DONE THAT, DON'T TEACH IT. THAT'S NOT YOUR WISDOM. YOU ARE HERE TO TEACH YOUR WISDOM.

NOW, THE GUIDE CARES VERY, VERY DEEPLY ABOUT THEIR FOLLOWERS. IT'S ALL ABOUT THE FOLLOWERS, BUT YOU ARE A GUIDE AND NOT A RUNNING MATE. YOU ARE GUIDING THEM ON THE PATH, NOT WALKING THE PATH WITH THEM LIKE A THREE-LEGGED RACE.

BRING THE AUTHORITY. "I'VE BEEN A CHANEL ALL MY LIFE. HERE'S WHAT I'VE LEARNED.", "THIS IS WHAT I'M SEEING, AND THIS IS MY PERSPECTIVE."
"HERE'S WHY THIS WORKS. HERE'S WHY THIS IS CLUNKY."
"YOU ASKED, I ANSWERED, THIS IS WHAT I KNOW WORKS.

if the marketing vibe of the generator is the ENERGY, the marketing vibe of the projector is the WISDOM.

for manifestors
the strategy for manifestors is "wait to inform"

THE WAITING IN THIS STRATEGY IS NOT "WAIT FOR THE CONDITIONS TO BE PERFECT AND THEN INFORM", IT MEANS WAIT TO ACT, UNTIL AFTER YOU'VE INFORMED.

MANIFESTORS IN THE NOT-SELF HAVE SUCH A HARD TIME WITH THIS. THEY SAY, "WHY DO I NEED TO TELL ANYONE WHAT I'M DOING EVER? THEY'RE JUST GOING TO SAY NO TO ME. IT'S A WASTE OF MY TIME". FOR ALL OF US, IT'S HARD TO LIVE OUR STRATEGY, YET IT'S THE KEY. SOMETHING THE MANIFESTOR HAS TO UNDERSTAND IS, YOU'RE NOT ASKING FOR ANYONE'S PERMISSION. TO USE RA URU HU'S ANALOGY, "BEFORE YOU PUSH THROUGH THE CROWD, SAY EXCUSE ME". THAT'S LITERALLY IT.

YOU'RE NOT ASKING FOR PERMISSION TO PASS. YOU ARE INFORMING PEOPLE *PEACEFULLY* THAT YOU ARE COMING THROUGH, AND THE CROWD PARTS LIKE THE RED SEA.

BLOWING UP ON SOMEONE IS NOT "INFORMING THEM". THE POINT IS TO INFORM BEFORE THE BLOWUP.

YOU HAVE TO UNDERSTAND, MANIFESTOR, THAT YOU ARE A BEING WITH AN ENORMOUS, ENORMOUS IMPACT ON THE WORLD. WHEN PEOPLE ARE INFORMED AS TO THE IMPACT THAT'S ABOUT TO TAKE PLACE, THEY CAN TRACE IT BACK TO YOU. WHEN IT JUST HAPPENS, WITHOUT ANY WARNING, THEY FEEL BLINDSIDED AND SUSPICIOUS. YOU HAVE TO TAKE THE TIME TO INFORM PEOPLE, FOR YOU, NOT FOR THEM.

When the Manifestor is aligned they feel Peace. When the manifestor is not aligned, or living in the not-self, they feel Anger. Something to note about the Manifestor and their not-self which is different than the other types, is that their own Anger really scares them.

THE GENERATOR CAN SIMMER IN FRUSTRATION, THE PROJECTOR CAN SIMMER IN BITTERNESS, AND THE REFLECTOR CAN SIMMER IN DISAPPOINTMENT, BUT THE **MANIFESTOR CANNOT SIMMER THAT LONG.**
IT BLOWS THE FUCK UP. IT BOILS THE FUCK OVER, AND THAT'S REALLY SCARY FOR THE MANIFESTOR, BECAUSE IT'S SO NOT THEM. IT'S SO NOT WHO THEY ARE HERE TO BE, AND THIS ANGER ALWAYS HAPPENS AS A RESULT OF NOT INFORMING PEOPLE SUFFICIENTLY OF YOUR NEEDS AND PLANS.

JOHNNY DEPP IS AN EMOTIONAL MANIFESTOR, AND HE'S A REALLY GOOD EXAMPLE OF SUCH A LOVER... UNTIL HE BLOWS UP. IN THE AMBER CASE WE HEARD HER DESCRIBE THESE FURIOUS MOMENTS OF HIS. EVERYONE IS RESPONSIBLE FOR 50% OF EVERY ARGUMENT THEY'RE IN, SO HIS BLOWUPS WOULD NOT HAVE BEEN AS SEVERE, HAD HE INFORMED SUFFICIENTLY.

THIS LOOKS LIKE TELLING SOMEONE WHAT YOUR NEEDS ARE, WHICH IS NOT ALWAYS EASY FOR THE SELF-SUFFICIENT MANIFESTOR TO DO.

Manifestors are the Samantha Joneses of the world.

MANIFESTORS CAN BE QUICK TO BLAME OTHERS FOR THE PROBLEM, THAT'S THEIR ANGER, WHEN THE ACTUAL ISSUE IS THAT MOST PEOPLE DO NOT KNOW OR CARE WHAT THE FUCK A MANIFESTOR IS! **YOU SHOULD ASSUME THAT NO ONE GIVES A SHIT ABOUT YOUR DESIGN EXCEPT FOR YOU, AND BECAUSE OF THIS YOU KNOW WHAT IT MEANS TO YOU AND CAN EXPLAIN IT.**

THIS IS THE PATH OF TEACHING. NO ONE GIVES A SHIT ABOUT YOUR EMOTIONAL DEFINITION OR YOUR GATE 58. YOU HAVE TO BE ABLE TO TELL THEM, IN HUMAN LANGUAGE, WHAT THAT MEANS ABOUT YOU. FOR EXAMPLE "MY MOODS AREN'T UP TO ME LIKE THEY ARE FOR OTHER PEOPLE" OR "WHEN I'M OUT OF ALIGNMENT, I CAN COME ACROSS AS A WORLD HATER WHEN I'M A WORLD LOVER".

THAT'S WHY WE'RE LEARNING THINGS PIECE BY PIECE. SO YOU CAN HAVE HUMAN DESIGN WISDOM, AND NOT HUMAN DESIGN KNOWLEDGE.

MANIFESTORS, YOU HAVE TO INFORM OTHERS. YOU HAVE TO ACCEPT THAT THE MOST ANGERING ASPECTS OF LIFE HAVE HAPPENED AS A RESULT OF NOT INFORMING THE OTHERS. IT'S NOT THEM, IT'S YOU. YOU ARE THE MINORITY AT 8%. **I RECOGNIZE THE TEMPTATION TO BURN THE BRIDGES CONNECTING YOU TO THE INEPT 92% OF THE WORLD, BUT YOU NEED US, AND WE NEED YOU TO INFORM US AND BOSS US AROUND. AN ANGRY BOSS INSPIRES EVERYONE TO QUIT. A PEACEFUL BOSS INSPIRES EVERYONE TO WORK.**

PEACE IS YOUR TRUTH. ANGER IS YOUR RESPONSIBILITY. THE SAME WAY A PROJECTORS BITTERNESS IS THEIR RESPONSIBILITY, A REFLECTORS DISAPPOINTMENT IS THEIR RESPONSIBILITY, AND A GENERATORS FRUSTRATION IS THEIR RESPONSIBILITY. YOU DIDN'T FOLLOW YOUR STRATEGY AND IT BIT YOU IN THE ASS. FORGIVE YOURSELF, AND USE IT AS A LESSON MOVING FORWARD.

marketing for manifestors

YOU WILL HAVE A DIFFERENT RELATIONSHIP TO MARKET RESEARCH THAN THE OTHER TYPES, AND WE DISCUSS MARKET RESEARCH IN MODULE 5 OF FUCKLESS.

THE WAY YOU WANT TO SPEAK TO YOUR CLIENT IS BY KEEPING THE "EXCUSE ME" METAPHOR IN MIND. YOU ARE MOVING FORWARD, INFORM THE AUDIENCE EXTREMELY WELL WHERE YOU ARE GOING AND WHY YOU ARE GOING THAT WAY, AND WHO IS INVITED WITH YOU AND WHAT THEY CAN EXPECT FROM YOU.

Your launch strategy could be as simple as that. Answering "Why? Who? What?" always in that order. Ask them if they need a "Where?" and "How?" and that's a wrap.

AND ALSO MAKING SURE EACH PIECE HAS BEEN DIGESTED BY THE CUSTOMER WITH A "PLEASE REACH OUT IN THIS SPECIFIC WAY IF YOU NEED MORE INFORMATION.

for reflectors

The strategy for a reflector is to wait a lunar cycle, and MAN, DO THEY HATE TO DO THIS. But they can either do it, or be disappointed.

THE ALIGNED REFLECTOR FEELS **SURPRISED**, AND THE **MISALIGNED** REFLECTOR FEELS DISAPPOINTED. CHARLOTTE YORK, ANYONE?

I COACHED A REFLECTOR FOR TEN MONTHS, WHO TRIED EVERY POSSIBLE WAY TO GET OUT OF SURRENDERING TO HER TIMING. IT DOES NOT WORK. IT FULL-STOP DOESN'T WORK.

THINGS TAKE A LONG TIME FOR REFLECTORS, AND **WHEN THEY FOLLOW THEIR STRATEGY, TRUSTING THAT IT WILL COME TOGETHER IN A LUNAR CYCLE, THEY FEEL PLEASANTLY SURPRISED WITH HOW EVERYTHING COMES TOGETHER! IT'S BETTER THAN THEY IMAGINED, AND IT ALL WORKED OUT! WOOT.**

BUT WHEN THEY REFUSE TO WAIT, COMPARING THEIR TIMELINE WITH THE TIMELINES OF LITERALLY ANYONE ELSE, IT'S A DISASTER, AND THE DISAPPOINTMENT CAN BE SO PROFOUND AND LONG LASTING THAT THEY NEVER WANT TO ATTEMPT SOMETHING AGAIN.

AS A REFLECTOR, YOU WILL BE EVERY DIFFERENT POTENTIAL HUMAN DESIGN TYPE THROUGHOUT THE COURSE OF A LUNAR CYCLE. YOU WILL HAVE MANIFESTOR DAYS WHERE YOU'RE LITERALLY THAT, GENERATOR AND MANI GEN DAYS, AND ALL TYPES OF PROJECTOR DAYS AS WELL. IF YOU TRUST YOUR TIMING, AND TRUST YOUR FLOW, YOU WILL SEE THAT IT ALL GETS DONE SURPRISINGLY EASILY.

IF YOU CAN'T TRUST YOUR FLOW; WHICH YOU LEARN HOW TO DO IN MODULE ONE, YOU CAN BOOK A $400 READING WITH STEPHEN REBOLLEDO WHERE YOU LEARN A COMPLEX SYSTEM FOR CALCULATING EXACTLY WHO YOU WILL BE AND ON WHAT DAY, AND MAKE A 28 DAY CONTENT CALENDAR TO CORRESPOND TO THAT. I SAT IN ON ONE OF THESE READINGS FOR MY 4/1 REFLECTOR CLIENT, AND IT WAS VERY, VERY COMPLICATED.

IT'S MUCH FASTER, AND MUCH EASIER TO JUST TRUST YOURSELF. MODULE FOUR OF FUCKLESS WILL SHOW YOU EXACTLY HOW TO DO THAT. IT'S SUCH A GOOD WORKSHOP. I'LL LET THE REVIEWS DO THE TALKING THOUGH, LATER

marketing for reflectors

AS A REFLECTOR, IT'S YOUR JOB TO SPEAK TO THE COLLECTIVE. YOU ARE A BIG FILTER FOR LIFE, THEREFORE YOUR RESEARCH NEEDS TO CAST A WIDE NET. YOU NEED TO STUDY ASTROLOGICAL TRANSITS AND UNDERSTAND WHERE THE COLLECTIVE IS AT, AND WHERE THE COLLECTIVE IS GOING.

A LOT OF PEOPLE UNDERSTAND THAT THE COLLECTIVE IS CHANGING, BUT THEY'RE RESISTANT, AND HOLDING ON. YOU NEED TO GUIDE THEM TO THE NEXT LEVEL. ASSURE THEM TIMES HAVE CHANGED, INSTAGRAM IS OVER, AND WE ARE MOVING TOWARD AN AUTHENTIC-CONTENT-ONLY MODEL. NO MORE GOOD-FOOT-FORWARD-ONLY PLATFORMS. THERE'S SOMETHING ABOUT THE CALM, CLEAR WAY THAT YOU LET PEOPLE KNOW THAT IT'S NOT ONLY THEM, IT'S ALL OF US, THAT CREATES AN INSANE AMOUNT OF TRUST.

BECOME KNOWN FOR KNOWING THE BIG PICTURE, AND MAKE A LIFESTYLE OF STUDYING THE BIG PICTURE. WE ONLY BEHAVE IN UNPREDICTABLE WAYS WHEN THE PLANETS BEHAVE IN PREDICTABLE WAYS. PREDICT THE PLANETS, AND SMOOTH THE TRANSITION.

REFLECTORS, YOU MUST TRUST YOUR TIMING. IF YOU HAVE BEEN TRYING TO MAKE THINGS HAPPEN IN LESS THAN A MONTH, PLEASE KNOW THAT IT'S NOT CLEAR TO OTHERS UNTIL IT'S CLEAR TO YOU. **IF A MIRROR IS DIRTY IN ONE SPOT, THE MIRROR IS DIRTY.** YOU'RE EITHER TOTALLY CLEAR, OR TOTALLY NOT. ALLOW THE CLARIFICATION PROCESS TO TAKE ITS 28 DAY CYCLE, TALK IT OUT WITH YOUR AUDIENCE WHILE BUILDING (BEFORE COMMITTING TO THE PROJECT) , AND AVOID THE DISAPPOINTMENT OF NOT KNOWING WTF YOU'RE EVEN SELLING.

YOU CAN EITHER START AND STOP OVER AND OVER AGAIN UNTIL YOU CONVINCE YOURSELF YOU'LL NEVER FINISH ANYTHING, OR YOU CAN WAIT A LUNAR CYCLE FOR THE NEXT PIECE OF THE PUZZLE TO COME FORWARD. IN THE MEANTIME, STUDY AND COMMUNICATE WITH THE COLLECTIVE.

STUDY SOCIAL MEDIA TRENDS, ASTROLOGICAL TRENDS, TRENDS IN GENERAL. IF YOU WANT TO DO SOMETHING TODAY, REFLECT ON THE LESSONS OF THE LAST 28 DAYS. KEEP A JOURNAL IN A PAPER BOOK, WITH DATES, SO THAT YOU CAN TRACK YOUR PROGRESS.
NEVER SET A LARGE GOAL WITH A ONE WEEK DEADLINE UNLESS YOU WANT TO BE DISAPPOINTED.

YOU ARE THE MOST HELD OF THE TYPES. YOU ARE LITERALLY HELD UP AND SUPPORTED BY EVERY PLANET AND EVERY PERSON. IT'S TIME TO ACKNOWLEDGE THAT WHERE YOU ARE WEAK, THEY ARE STRONG, AND THAT STRENGTH CAN BE YOURS IF YOU WAIT A LUNAR CYCLE AND ALLOW LIFE TO FEED YOU, WORK FOR YOU, AND GIVE YOU A DAY AS EACH AND EVERY TYPE TO GET IT ALL DONE.

AND DON'T CONFUSE PHYSICAL REST WITH MENTAL REST. EACH ARE NEEDED.

Use the data of your reflections, let us know how you came to these conclusions.
"After examining the evidence I've found that"
"According to my research" ;)
"After reflecting on the situation I found that"
"After polling my audience for the last month I learned that"
"This is what's really going on here"

HINDSIGHT IS 20/20 FOR YOU REFLECTORS, THERE IS ALWAYS SOMETHING YOU'RE CLEAR ABOUT. IT'S BEHIND YOU. YOU ARE CLARIFYING WHAT'S CURRENTLY BOTHERING YOU. BUT YOU'VE ALREADY CLARIFIED SOMETHING IN THE PAST.

Pro Tip: Use your audience's words right back to them. If they said "I struggle with making the time", when you're ready to sell say "I know you struggle with making the time

QUESTIONS TO ANSWER:
WHAT HAVE YOU RECENTLY CLARIFIED?

WHO CAN THIS SERVE?

business audit:

For each and every human design type, the not-self is your portal to creation. Your portal to wealth.

GENERATORS AND MANIFESTING GENERATORS, YOUR FRUSTRATION WILL DRIVE YOU TO CREATE!

MANIFESTORS, YOUR ANGER WILL DRIVE YOU TO CREATE!

PROJECTORS, YOUR BITTERNESS WILL DRIVE YOU TO CREATE!

REFLECTORS, YOUR DISAPPOINTMENT WILL DRIVE YOU TO CREATE!

But these not self themes will always hold you back in business as well. Wherever the not-self feeling shows up in your business, that's the aspect that needs to be scaled. That's the aspect that needs to be grown. You are not meant to live in the not-self. If you are always frustrated at your job as a generator, then you need to switch it up...

IF YOUR JOB IS BEING A MOM AND YOU ARE ALWAYS FRUSTRATED, IT'S BECAUSE YOU ARE NOT RESPONDING TO THE CHILDREN. YOU ARE INITIATING. THE PROJECTORS, REFLECTORS, AND MANIFESTORS CAN DO THIS SAME PARENTING AUDIT. YOUR PARENTING STRATEGY IS *STILL* YOUR HUMAN DESIGN STRATEGY.

74

ask yourself these questions

for a full business audit! Insert your not-self theme in each and every question.

WHERE ARE YOU CURRENTLY FEELING *INSERT NOT SELF FEELING HERE* IN YOUR BUSINESS?

WHAT WOULD *INSERT TRUE SELF FEELING HERE* LOOK LIKE FOR YOU IN THIS AREA OF BUSINESS?

HOW IS THIS *NOT SELF FEELING* GREAT?

WHAT'S NOT PERFECT YET?

WHAT NEEDS TO BE DONE TO MAKE THINGS SATISFYING/ SUCCESSFUL/PEACEFUL/SURPRISING FOR YOU HERE?

WHAT MUST BE STOPPED TO MAKE THINGS HOW YOU WANT IT?

HOW CAN YOU ENJOY IT?

Good job! That was the biggest Human Design concept to get. Go write your type and strategy on your Human Design chart page, and come share what that means to you in our Fuckless chat. To articulate it is to master it.

trust
yourself

success patterning
marketing
vulnerability
HD Profile

your success pattern.

WHEN WE GET TO THE TRUST MODULE OF FUCKLESS, WE'LL DO A REALLY SPECIFIC FORMULA FOR BRINGING TRUST AND REMOVING THE BARRIERS TO TRUST, IT'S AWESOME, BUT FOR NOW WHAT WE WANT YOU TO DO IS COME TO TRUST IN YOUR UNIQUE EXPRESSION OF SUCCESS.

Each of us has a success pattern that is unique to us, and meant to be honored.

WHEN WE LOOK AT OUR SUCCESS PATTERN OBJECTIVELY, AS AN OBSERVER, WE SEE THAT THERE ARE ALWAYS CERTAIN COMPONENTS THAT CONTRIBUTE TO OUR SUCCESS. WHEN WE UNDERSTAND THESE COMPONENTS, WE CAN ADD THE MISSING PIECES ANY TIME WE ARE STRUGGLING, AND WE CAN ALSO RECOGNIZE THESE CRUCIAL LANDMARKS ON THE WAY TO SUCCESS.

THIS IS SOMETHING WE DO IN ONE OF THE DAYS OF MY 40 DAY MONEY WORKSHOP, BREAKING BROKE 2.0, AND A VARIATION OF THIS IN MESOTERICA AS WELL. IT'S ALWAYS USEFUL.

IT'S SO IMPORTANT TO KNOW YOUR UNIQUE SUCCESS PATTERN BECAUSE SOMETIMES, CRUCIAL ASPECTS TO YOUR UNIQUE SUCCESS MIGHT SEEM TOXIC, OR BAD TO SOMEONE ELSE'S DEFINITION, AND IT'S NOT. IT'S JUST NOT RIGHT FOR THEM.

FOR EXAMPLE, MY UNIQUE SUCCESS PATTERN IS VERY ON BRAND FOR THE GENERATOR. I ALWAYS HAVE A MOMENT WHERE I REALIZE: "SHIT. NO ONE CAN HELP ME, I HAVE TO DO IT ALL BY MYSELF."

I REALIZED IT DOING THIS BOOK, THAT NO ONE CAN DO THE LAYOUT AS PERFECTLY AS I WANT IT, AND I WILL NEED TO DO THE LAYOUT FOR THIS BABY INSTEAD OF HOPING SOMEONE ELSE WILL DO IT. I REALIZED IT WHEN WE WERE BUILDING OUR APP AND I FOUND OUT THE DEVELOPER HAD BEEN SCAMMING ME. I HAD TO LEARN HOW TO BUILD AN APP, AND BUILD IT IN JUST TWO WEEKS. OH YEAH, AND MY HUSBAND TORE HIS MENISCUS THAT WEEK TOO! SO I HAD TO HAUL FIREWOOD, WATCH KIDS 24/7, AND DO THE DINNER DISHES THE WHOLE TIME AS WELL. LUCKILY, AT THAT POINT I KNEW IT WAS A PART OF MY SUCCESS PATTERN, AND BECAUSE KNOWING IS THE FIRST STEP TOWARDS TRUSTING, I DIDN'T LOSE MY SHIT TOO MUCH. IF I SEE THE MILESTONE OF "SHIT. NO ONE CAN HELP ME, I HAVE TO DO IT ALL BY MYSELF.", I KNOW SUCCESS IS JUST AROUND THE CORNER.

GOOD THING I HIRED A COACH FOR 13K TO HELP ME UNWIND THIS "TOXIC BELIEF" THAT NO ONE CAN HELP ME. GOOD THING I HIRED A BUNCH OF PEOPLE TO DO NOTHING, BASICALLY, WHILE ATTEMPTING TO REMOVE AN INTEGRAL PART OF MY SUCCESS PATTERN. DON'T GET ME WRONG, I BELIEVE IN DELEGATING, BUT ONLY THE THINGS OTHER PEOPLE CAN DO BETTER THAN YOU. I CAN'T EDIT, BUT I CAN WRITE. I CAN'T FORMAT A BOOK FOR KDP, BUT I CAN DO THE LAYOUT TO PERFECTION, EXACTLY THE WAY I WANT IT.

ANOTHER KEY ASPECT OF MY SUCCESS PATTERN IS A DEADLINE, AND FOR A WHILE THERE I WANTED TO BE ON THE BEYONCE CREATIVE SCHEDULE WHERE I KEPT MY PROJECTS SECRET, AND WORKED ON THEM UNTIL THEY WERE DONE BEFORE "DROPPING" THEM, WHENEVER THEY WERE DONE.

THAT'S SO KEY TO HER SUCCESS, BUT IF I DON'T HAVE A DEADLINE, I DON'T HAVE A DEADLINE. THE PROJECT CAN STRETCH ON INFINITELY UNTIL I FEEL LIKE IT'S PERFECT, WHICH IS NEVER. A GOOD, STRONG, IMPOSSIBLE-SEEMING DEADLINE IS ALWAYS A RECIPE FOR SUCCESS FOR THIS CAPRICORN RIGHT HERE! NOW I KNOW, FROM EXPERIENCE, THAT IF I WANT SUCCESS, I HAVE TO SET A DEADLINE FOR IT AND STICK TO IT. ONE EXTENSION BECOMES A HUNDRED EXTENSIONS.

THE POET, MARY OLIVER SAYS

"attention is the beginning of devotion."

YOUR SACRED SUCCESS PATTERN IS HERE TO HOLD YOU, TO LOVE YOU, AND TO SHOW YOU YOUR WAY. NOBODY ELSE'S SUCCESS WAY MATTERS OR IS RELEVANT HERE, JUST YOURS. BY PUTTING THIS LITTLE BIT OF ATTENTION ONTO YOUR UNIQUE SUCCESS PATTERN, YOUR DEVOTION TO IT AND IT'S DEVOTION TO YOU WILL START TO UNFOLD, AND I'M SO, SO HAPPY FOR YOU

objective success worksheet.

GRADUATES OF MY TEACHER TRAINING WHEELS: REINVENTED WILL
RECOGNIZE THIS PROCESS AND EXACTLY WHAT WE'RE DOING HERE ;)

WHEN WAS THE LAST TIME YOU FELT TRULY SUCCESSFUL?

WHERE WERE YOU?

WHAT HAD HAPPENED TO MAKE YOU FEEL THIS WAY?

WHAT DOES THE FEELING OF SUCCESS FEEL LIKE TO YOU?

WHERE IN YOUR BODY DO YOU FEEL IT?

HOW WOULD YOU DRAW IT? DRAW OR DESCRIBE?

WHEN WAS THE FIRST TIME YOU EVER FELT THIS WAY?

WHERE WERE YOU?

WHAT HAD HAPPENED TO MAKE YOU FEEL THIS WAY?

RETURN TO THE FEELING, AND HOW YOU WOULD DRAW IT.

Briefly list three other times in life you felt this way, returning to the way you would draw the feeling in between each memory.

1. where were you?
2. what made you feel this way?
3. Return to the feeling.

1. where were you?
2. what made you feel this way?
3. Return to the feeling.

1. where were you?
2. what made you feel this way?
3. Return to the feeling?

What do you notice about your unique success pattern in each of these memories?

Are there any other patterns, besides the success feeling, that you notice in these memories?

By any chance, had you applied your strategy unsconsciously? Not necessarily in the execution of the task, but in regards to how the task came to you in the first place?

What does this tell you about the success pattern that is currently unfolding for you?

How can you best support yourself in your currently unfolding success pattern?

What extra components are necessary for your unique expression of success? (For me, a deadline!)

Now that we've done our internal work, let's move it to the marketplace.

marketing

ONE OF THE MAIN MYTHS OF MARKETING IS THAT MARKETING IS CONVINCING SOMEONE TO BUY SOMETHING. THIS COULD NOT BE FURTHER FROM THE TRUTH, YOU CAN'T CONVINCE ANYONE TO BUY ANYTHING. AND THE MORE YOU TRY TO CONVINCE SOMEONE TO BUY SOMETHING, THE SLEAZIER IT SEEMS. IF YOUR PRODUCT IS VERY CHEAP, SOMETIMES PEOPLE WILL BUY SIMPLY TO "RESPECT THE HUSTLE", BUT THEY'RE NOT GOING TO DO THIS MORE THAN ONCE, AND IT'S UNSUSTAINABLE.

Marketing is making the customer feel seen and heard. That's it.

IN A MARKETPLACE THAT IS JAM PACKED WITH PRODUCTS, THE BIGGEST QUESTION THE CUSTOMER HAS IS,

"HOW DO I KNOW IF THIS IS RIGHT FOR ME? EVERYONE SAYS THEIR PRODUCT IS SO GREAT, HOW DO I KNOW IF THIS IS RIGHT FOR ME?"
IF YOU CANNOT PHYSICALLY SEE, AND PHYSICALLY HEAR EVERY CUSTOMER YOU HAVE, UNLESS YOU'RE IN THE ABSOLUTE BEGINNING STAGES OF YOUR BUSINESS, HOW DO YOU MAKE A CONGREGATION FEEL SEEN AND HEARD?

THE FIRST WAY IS TO ASK QUESTIONS, LOADS AND LOADS OF QUESTIONS. THIS IS SOMETHING WE COVER IN THE SEED LAUNCHING MODULE (4), AS WELL AS THE MARKET RESEARCH MODULE (5), THE SALES TRIGGERS MODULE (1), AND MOST IMPORTANTLY IN THE DATA MODULE (9) THIS IS SOMETHING I HAVE BEEN STUDYING FOR YEARS, TAKING EVERY ANGLE FROM PRODUCT DEVELOPMENT, TO PUBLIC SPEAKING, TO HOSTAGE NEGOTIATION IN ORDER TO MORE DEEPLY UNDERSTAND. SO PLEASE, PLEASE DON'T LET THIS OPEN AND SHUT THE BOOK FOR YOU WHEN IT COMES TO ASKING CUSTOMERS QUESTIONS, OR MARKETING, OR HUMAN DESIGN. LET IT BE A SIGNIFICANT MILESTONE ON A BIG JOURNEY.

IF YOU ENDED EVERY POST IN A QUESTION, IT WOULD BOOST YOUR ENGAGEMENT UNCANNILY.

IF YOU WANT SOMEONE TO TEXT YOU BACK, ASK THEM A QUESTION.

IF YOU'RE STUCK, OR THE DEVELOPMENT AT ANY STAGE IS TAKING TOO LONG, ASK YOUR AUDIENCE A QUESTION.

YOU'RE READING THIS AS A BOOK, AND NOT GETTING IT AS A MASTERCLASS BECAUSE I ASKED YOU THREE DIFFERENT TIMES, IN THREE DIFFERENT PLACES WHICH YOU WOULD PREFER. TIKTOK, MY NEWSLETTER LIST, AND MY SCHOOL.

YOU'RE GETTING FUCKLESS TIME RELEASED THE WAY THAT IT IS BECAUSE I ASKED THE FIRST 50 PEOPLE WHO TOOK THE WORKSHOP AT THE END IF THEY WOULD PREFER WEEKLY, OR TWICE A MONTH WORK.

AT THE END OF EVERY NEWSLETTER I SEND, I ASK YOU QUESTIONS. THIS IS TO MAKE SURE YOU'RE GETTING RESULTS, AND NOT JUST READING MINE AND BEING LIKE "OH WOW, GREAT FOR YOU.".

**Projectors, ask questions.
Generators, ask LOADS of questions, like you're talking to a friend.
Reflectors, ask LOADS of questions.
The more response, the more accurate the view of the collective.
Manifestors, you don't need to ask as many questions.**

WHAT YOU DO NEED TO ASK IS IF PEOPLE ARE CLEAR. IF THEY'RE TOTALLY CLEAR. IF THERE'S ANY WAY YOU CAN INFORM THEM FURTHER OR IF THEY GET IT.

REMEMBER, IT'S NEVER INCONVENIENT TO SOLVE A PROBLEM. SOLVING A PROBLEM IS MAKING A SALE. SOLVING A PROBLEM IS GOOD ADVERTISING. PERIOD.

THE MORE QUESTIONS YOU ASK, THE MORE YOUR CUSTOMER FEELS SEEN AND HEARD.

vulnerability

Vulnerability is the seed of strength. That "weakness" is the seed that all strength sprouts from.

THE MYTH IS THAT IF YOU TELL PEOPLE YOU'RE NOT PERFECT, AND YOU HAVE PROBLEMS, THAT THEY WON'T HIRE YOU. NOTHING COULD BE FURTHER FROM THE TRUTH.

LIFE IS A STRUGGLE, AND IF YOU DON'T STRUGGLE, YOU'RE NOT LIVING LIFE.

THE PURPOSE OF A TEACHER IS TO SAVE THE STUDENT TIME, BUT HOW CAN YOU SAVE THEM TIME IF YOU'RE NOT BEING CLEAR THAT YOU HAVE STRUGGLED, AND STRUGGLE NOW. LETTING YOUR CUSTOMER KNOW THAT YOU'RE NOT PERFECT, AND YOU WRANGLE WITH THESE ISSUES MAKE THEM FEEL SEEN.

IF YOUR WORK IS ANY GOOD, IT'S GOING TO BE CHALLENGING TO REMEMBER TO APPLY IT. THAT'S REALLY WHAT MAKES MY WORK DIFFERENT.

*I KNOW YOU KNOW, I KNOW YOU KNOW TO DRINK WATER. I KNOW YOU'VE PROBABLY READ YOUR WHOLE HUMAN DESIGN CHART AT SOME POINT. I KNOW YOU KNOW YOU NEED REST, AND BOUNDARIES, AND AN ARSENAL OF SPIRITUAL PRACTICES YOU'VE PICKED UP OVER THE YEARS. I KNOW YOU KNOW, BUT I KNOW THAT THE HARDEST PART FOR ME, AFTER ALL THESE YEARS, IS REMEMBERING THAT I KNOW. YEP, THAT FORGETTING IS A FUNCTION OF THE MANIPURA CHAKRA, AND THAT'S WHY IT'S SUCH A CONSISTENT PAIN IN YOUR ASS. TO BE ON THE OTHER SIDE OF SOMETHING YOU STRUGGLED WITH FOR MONTHS AND **THEN REALIZE THE SOLUTION WAS SOMETHING YOU KNEW THE ANSWER TO THE WHOLE TIME.***

THIS LITERALLY JUST HAPPENED TO ME. SOMEONE I KNEW WELL STOLE $14,000 FROM ME IN A BREACH OF TRUST. IT TAKES A LONG TIME TO GET STOLEN MONEY BACK FROM AN UNCOOPERATIVE PARTNER. I KNEW HER, BUT NOT WELL ENOUGH TO NOT TAKE HER TO COURT FOR IT. I HAD BEEN TRYING TO BE "PROFESSIONAL" THE WHOLE TIME AND I JUST COULD NOT LET IT GO. I HAD TRIED TO NOT SAY ANYTHING, NOT COMMUNICATE AT ALL AND LET MY HUSBAND HANDLE IT, AND AS A RESULT THE CASE HAD BEEN STALEMATED FOR MONTHS.

FINALLY, WHILE WRITING THIS ACTUALLY, I FINALLY SENT HER AN EMAIL AND JUST LET THE FEELINGS FLY. IT FUCKING SUCKS TO BE STOLEN FROM BY SOMEONE YOU TRUSTED, WORKED REALLY HARD TO SATISFY, AND OVERDELIVERED. **I SPOKE FROM MY HEART AND THE CASE WAS RESOLVED WITHIN 3 HOURS.**

IT WAS ONLY AFTER I SENT IT THAT I REALIZED I HAD KNOWN, LIKE REALLY KNOWN THIS ANSWER SINCE 2016. THE PROBLEM WAS, I FORGOT TO USE IT. THE ANSWER I HAD FORGOTTEN WAS:

YOU CAN'T EVER FORGIVE WITHOUT BEING HONEST ABOUT HOW MUCH SOMETHING HURT. ANGER IS SADNESS DOWN THE ROAD. ACKNOWLEDGING YOUR ANGER DOES NOTHING TO RESOLVE IT. ACKNOWLEDGING YOUR SADNESS, AND HONORING IT WITH THE TRUTH IS THE ONLY WAY TO MOVE FORWARD.

A SIMPLE PATTERN IN MY BUSINESS IS THAT I AM ALWAYS VULNERABLE ABOUT FORGETTING TO DO THE WORK, AND 70% OF WHAT I DO IS GIVE PRACTICAL SOLUTIONS, LIKE A COLORING BOOK, TO HELP YOU REMEMBER WHAT YOU'VE LEARNED, SO YOU CAN APPLY IT WHEN YOU NEED TO.

The vulnerability is "I struggle to remember too."

THE MARKETING SIDE OF VULNERABILITY IS THAT WHEN I TOLD MY STORY, YOU REMEMBERED A STORY OF YOUR OWN WHEN YOU HAD THE ANSWER THE WHOLE TIME AND FORGOT.

THIS MAKES YOU FEEL SEEN.

THIS MAKES YOU FEEL HEARD.

WE HAVEN'T TALKED, BUT YOU'RE NO LONGER WORRIED THAT THIS WORKSHOP WILL GO INTO YOUR INBOX, WHERE IT WILL SIT, COLLECTING DUST, BECAUSE YOU DON'T EVEN REMEMBER THAT YOU BOUGHT IT.

I'VE BEEN THERE TOO! WE HAVE AN APP FOR THAT.

BY SHARING YOUR RAW STORIES, VULNERABLY, YOU ARE EXPOSING YOUR ACHILLES HEEL TO THE WORLD. THE INTERESTING THING ABOUT DOING THIS IS THAT WHEN YOU SHOW SOMEONE YOUR WEAK SPOT, YOU ALSO SHOW THEM THEIR WEAK SPOT. VULNERABILITY INVITES VULNERABILITY. A COMMENT I GET ALL THE TIME IS

"I feel seen."

Human Design: Lesson Two

Profile

your profile

The reason I constantly flaunt my mistakes is because I have a 6/3 profile in human design

YOUR PROFILE IS TWO NUMBERS, REPRESENTING YOUR CONSCIOUS SUN, AND YOUR UNCONSCIOUS SUN. **IN HUMAN DESIGN THIS IS KIND OF LIKE YOUR SUN SIGN AND YOUR MOON** SIGN. THE SUN SIGN IS WHAT YOU KNOW ABOUT YOURSELF, AND THE MOON SIGN IS YOUR NEEDS.

MY SUN SIGN IS CAPRICORN, WHICH MEANS I KNOW THAT I LIKE TO BE IN CONTROL, AND START AND FINISH EVERY PROJECT, INCLUDING THE YEAR ;) MY MOON SIGN IS IN PISCES, WHICH MEANS I GET ADDICTED TO EVERYTHING AND DON'T THINK I'M ADDICTED. IT ALSO MEANS I ABSORB MY SURROUNDINGS AND MUST KEEP THEM PRISTINE. THERE IS NO WAY TO CLEAN CONTAMINATED WATER, YOU JUST HAVE TO DUMP THE GLASS OUT, CLEAN IT, AND DO BETTER NEXT TIME. I HAVE TO SHAKE OFF THE SURROUNDINGS COMPLETELY, AND TRY AGAIN.

THE FIRST NUMBER OF YOUR PROFILE IS WHAT YOU KNOW ABOUT YOURSELF. FOR EXAMPLE, MY 6 REPRESENTS MY ROLE MODEL. I'M PRETTY FAR UP MY OWN ASS ON A BAD DAY, SO I COULD RESONATE WITH THIS, ALTHOUGH I DID NOT REALIZE THAT THE RECOGNITION FOR THE ROLE MODEL REALLY COMES AT 50+, SO I'M NOT LATE TO THE PARTY, I'M HERE FOR THE LONG HAUL.

THE 3 REPRESENTS THE MARTYR, WHICH IS SOMETHING I DID NOT KNOW ABOUT MYSELF. THE MARTYR MAKES MISTAKES FOR LIFE. THE SIX LINE LIVES AS A THREE LINE FOR THE FIRST THIRTY YEARS, AND THEN IF YOU WERE A 6/2 , LIKE MY HUSBAND, YOU COULD JUST LIKE, MOVE ON OUT OF THAT PHASE. HOWEVER, BECAUSE I HAVE THAT 3 ON THE OTHER SIDE OF MY PROFILE, **I AM HERE TO MAKE MISTAKES ALL LIFE LONG.**

before I realized this, I was always thinking that one day I could just be perfect and not make any mistakes.

I TRIED TO HIDE MY MISTAKES, WHICH ONLY MADE ME MAKE BIGGER ONES. THEN I TRIED TO NOT SHOW ANY OF MY WORK UNTIL IT WAS PERFECT, WHICH MEANT THAT I DIDN'T MAKE ANY WORK. THE 6/3 IS LIKE AN INVENTOR, AND INVENTORS KNOW WHAT DOESN'T WORK JUST AS WELL AS THEY KNOW WHAT DOES WORK. THAT DATA IS THEIR PAYCHECK, AND THERE'S NO MISTAKES, NO MENTORS ON THAT PATH REALLY. NO MATTER WHAT, THE 6/3 AND THE INVENTOR HAS TO LEARN BY TRIAL AND ERROR.

WHEN I WAS TOLD THIS ABOUT MYSELF BY ZSUZSI I WAS LIKE, "TAKE IT BACK." BASICALLY. LEARNING THAT I WOULD MAKE PUBLIC MISTAKES FOR MY WHOLE LIFE I WAS LIKE. "TAKE IT BACK!" . THEN SHE TOLD ME I HAD THE HIGHEST EARNING POTENTIAL OF ANY OF THE OTHER PROFILE LINES. I'M VERY MONEY MINDED (NOW), SO I PERKED UP A BIT AND HAVE LEANED ON MY PROFILE EVER SINCE THEN.

YOUR UNIQUE WAY OF SHARING YOUR JOURNEY IN THE MARKET, AND MAKING YOUR CUSTOMERS FEEL SEEN AND HEARD, IS GOING TO HAVE TWO MAIN COMPONENTS FROM YOUR HUMAN DESIGN CHART THAT WORK IN YOUR FAVOR. YOUR PROFILE, AND YOUR MESSAGING WHICH WE DO IN MODULE 3
.
I AM NOT A HUMAN DESIGN EXPERT, AND I'M PROUD OF THAT. I THINK IT'S INCREDIBLY EASY TO GET LOST IN THE SAUCE AND LOSE THE PRACTICAL APPLICATION IN THE DATA. I'M ALSO NOT AN EXPERT IN ASTROLOGY, BECAUSE I FEEL THE SAME WAY ABOUT IT. TOO MUCH TO REMEMBER, TOO LITTLE TO APPLY. BUT WHAT I DO IS TAKE ALL THE INFORMATION IN, LOCATE THE PIECES THAT WERE MOST A HA, AND TEACH THAT. FOR EXAMPLE, SUN SIGN, MOON SIGN, RISING SIGN. AND WE WILL GET TO RISING SIGN IN FUCKLESS.

NOW, I AM A MARKETING EXPERT, AND I AM DOUBLE THAT ON AUTHENTICITY, WHICH IS WHAT THIS WORKSHOP IS REALLY ABOUT. HUMAN DESIGN IS A COOL TOOL TO MAKE THIS HAPPEN, BUT IT'S ULTIMATELY JUST A TOOL IN THE HAND.

THE BUILDER IS AUTHENTICITY, AND THE BUILDING IS MARKETING. THE HUMAN DESIGN IS THE TOOL THAT CONNECTS THE TWO.

Human Design homework:

I COULD EXPLAIN EACH AND EVERY PROFILE LINE TO YOU, BUT 70% OF THAT WOULDN'T MEAN ANYTHING TO YOU AND I'M NOT THAT GOOD AT IT, TBH. **WHAT I'M GOING TO HAVE YOU DO INSTEAD IS GET YOUR PROFILE NUMBERS, AND HEAD TO YOUTUBE. TYPE IN THOSE NUMBERS, FOR EXAMPLE "6/3" AND "RICHARD BEAUMONT". NOW HE IS AN EXPERT ON NOT JUST THE INDIVIDUAL NUMBERS, BUT EACH PROFILE AS WELL.**

Baby, when I say I cried watching my six minute video, I fuckin' CRIED.

MORE SO IN THIS VIDEO THAN BY GETTING THIS INFO FROM NOT ONE, BUT TWO HUMAN DESIGN SPECIALISTS, 1:1. WHEN HE EXPLAINED TO ME CALMLY ON YOUTUBE THAT I'M CHAOTIC, ALWAYS HAVE BEEN, ALWAYS WILL BE AND THAT'S OKAY - THE TEARS OF FEELING SEEN AND HEARD JUST ROLLED DOWN MY PRETTY LITTLE FACE.

I WANT THAT FOR YOU. SO LET'S TAKE OUR PROFILE NUMBERS TO MR. BEAUMONT ON YOUTUBE, AND NOT GET DISTRACTED WITH LOOKING UP EVERY OTHER PERSON'S CHART. WE CAN DO THIS LATER, BUT RIGHT NOW YOU NEED TO FOCUS ON THIS. A SPONGE CAN ONLY ABSORB SO MUCH AT A TIME.

I am a   /

This means that I:

I now understand that I:

I was aware that I:

But I wasn't aware that I:

Now I want to:

And I think this could be really useful in how I tell my story because:

Who else can this serve?

I'LL GIVE YOU MORE HUMAN DESIGN MARKETING HACKS AT THE END OF THIS BOOK, BUT IT'S REALLY IMPORTANT THAT WE DON'T OVERSATURATE THE HD SPONGE. BY ALL MEANS, FAFO.

BUT IT'S GONNA TAKE A LOOOOOOOONG TIME TO FIND OUT, AKA THE FRUSTRATION/DISAPPOINTMENT/ BITTERNESS/ANGER WHEN YOU GET TO THE BOTTOM OF THE RESEARCH PILE AND REALIZE NONE OF IT MEANS ANYTHING TO YOU AND YOU DON'T REMEMBER ANY OF IT. KNOWLEDGE YOU DON'T APPLY BECOMES IMAGINARY KNOWLEDGE, WHICH EVENTUALLY MAKES YOU SICK.

BY ALL MEANS, FAFO. FUCK AROUND AND FIND OUT. BUT I AM HERE TO PREVENT PEOPLE FROM MAKING THE SAME MISTAKES SO MANY OTHERS, AND I, HAVE MADE. SO MAYBE YOU'LL LISTEN

Now, for the last piece of trust....

Why should you trust me to guide you on this?

**You shouldn't! That's the short answer.
You should prove everything to yourself.**

Does what I'm saying make sense to you?
Have these concepts resonated?
Are you seeing results?
I'm here to lead by example. Do you think I'm authentic, or
do you think I'm faking it?
You're reading a marketing strategy.
Do you think my marketing is bad?
Useless?
Annoying?
Not serving?
You're IN my launch. Do you think launching is annoying to
the customer?
Or are you having a good time and learning things here?

IF YOUR ANSWERS HERE MAKE IT SEEM LIKE I MIGHT BE
#GOALS IN THE AUTHENTICITY AND MARKETING
DEPARTMENT, AT LEAST FOR NOW,

let me tell you something I have that no one else has...

An objective formula for authenticity. The ONLY one that exists

THE ONLY METHOD THAT GUARANTEES YOU WILL BE AUTHENTIC LIKE YOU AND NOT AUTHENTIC LIKE ME. IT IS A MATHEMATICAL EQUATION FOR AUTHENTICITY, AND A PRACTICAL APPLICATION OF THAT TO THE MARKETPLACE. **IF I SEEM CRAZY CONFIDENT**, IT'S BECAUSE I'M NOT RESTING ON HOPE. I'M RESTING ON MATH. I KNOW, THAT AS SURELY AS 1+1=2 (WHICH IS ABOUT THE MOST ADVANCED MATH THAT I KNOW), THAT **IF YOU TAKE EACH STEP GIVEN, YOU WILL REACH OBJECTIVE AUTHENTICITY.**

THIS IS THE MAGIC OF THE ENNEAGRAM, WHICH ONLY I TEACH WHEN IT COMES TO ITS APPLICATION IN BUSINESS. PLEASE GO RESEARCH IF ANYONE ELSE IS DOING THIS, OR DOING IT CHEAPER FOR REAL, AND TELL ME! BUT MAKE SURE WHEN YOU RESEARCH "AUTHENTICITY WORKSHOP" THAT THE TEACHER IS SAYING IT'S OBJECTIVE AUTHENTICITY, AND NOT JUST HOW THEY MANAGED TO BECOME AUTHENTIC, BECAUSE THAT WON'T WORK FOR ANYONE BUT THEM.

AND WHEN YOU RESEARCH THE ENNEAGRAM, MAKE SURE IT DOES NOT SAY "ENNEAGRAM OF PERSONALITY" ANYWHERE, BECAUSE THAT'S SOME BOBO SHIT. ALSO MAKE SURE IT'S IN RELATION TO BUSINESS.

I'M THE FIRST ONE, AND THE ONLY ONE. THAT'S MY POSITIONING.

YOU EITHER TRUST SOMEONE OR YOU DON'T, AND WE TALK ABOUT TRUST MUCH DEEPER IN FUCKLESS MODULE 4. I NEVER HAVE TO LOOK UP WHAT MODULE THINGS ARE IN BECAUSE IT'S AN OBJECTIVE, MATHEMATICAL, MAGICAL FORMULA AND I ALWAYS KNOW EXACTLY WHERE MY STUDENTS ARE, AND EXACTLY WHERE THEY'RE GOING. THAT'S INTELLIGENCE, KNOWING WHERE YOU ARE, AND IT'S WHY MY SCHOOL IS BEST IN SHOW.

YOU CAN LEARN ABOUT THE ENNEAGRAM MORE, OF COURSE, IN MY SCHOOL. PREVIEWS ON THE FREE VERSION, FULL LENGTH ON THE PAID. THERE ARE MANY MORE BOOKS LIKE THIS ON THERE.

reviews from last round:

Fuckless is a more than a course in becoming who you truly are, it's a revealing of who you've always been. This is a lifting of veils, a marriage to who you were... underneath. But don't get it twisted... it is work & you have to be the one to do it. Onami is a powerful guide who understands that we are in the ocean together. Touching depths with lighting. The only limits are the ones we give ourselves. We become fuckless when we open ourselves to each other. Thank you for a wave I won't forget.

 6

I feel that mushrooms are like the restart button for the heart. I haven't done them in years but I must have been overdue because that's what Fuckless has felt like. Peeling back the layers and learning to love myself all over again. I'd do it again. The results this time around... well it's not that who I am has changed so much as the way I see myself and the way I love myself has changed. I feel more like myself and I like myself more. (edited)

 2   1   1   1

be yourself
and know that's enough

sales blocks
audiences
case studies
HD Brand
HD Authority
reviews

you came here to do a thing.

YOU DIDN'T COME HERE TO DO A SECRET THING AND IMPACT NO ONE. YOU CAME HERE TO CHANGE THE WORLD, AND POSITIVELY SHIFT THE LIVES OF EVERY PERSON WHO SIGNED A SOUL CONTRACT WITH YOU. THESE SOUL CONTRACTORS ARE YOUR BUYERS. BUT THEY CANNOT BECOME BUYERS, AND THEY CANNOT HEAL UNTIL YOU BECOME A SELLER.

I'VE BEEN TEACHING A WORKSHOP ON MONEY BLOCKS FOR SEVEN YEARS NOW, THAT'S MY WORKSHOP BREAKING BROKE 2.0, AND YOU SHOULD DEFINITELY START THAT TODAY IF YOU HAVEN'T YET. **I HAVE HEARD EVERY POSSIBLE STORY ABOUT WHY PEOPLE FEEL THEY CAN'T SELL, AND IT'S ALWAYS ROOTED IN THE SAME HUGE BLOCK.**

THE BIGGEST BLOCK IS NOT THE FEAR OF WHAT OTHER PEOPLE WILL THINK.

THE BIGGEST BLOCK IS NOT FEAR OF ANNOYING YOUR CUSTOMER.

THE BIGGEST BLOCK IS NOT FEAR OF FALLING OUT OF SPIRITUAL LINE.

The biggest block is fear that other people will judge you for selling your unique gifts as much as you have judged others for selling theirs.

THAT'S RIGHT, YOUR BIGGEST BLOCK TO SELLING IS JUDGING OTHER PEOPLE FOR SELLING

IN MY WORKSHOP JELLY, WHICH IS AN EXPRESS OPENING OF THE VISSUDA CHAKRA (FOR ALL CHAKRAS, YOU CAN DO MY TEACHER TRAINING, WHEELS: REINVENTED), WE TEACH A REALLY SIMPLE FORMULA FOR LOCATING YOUR BIGGEST BUSINESS BLOCK.

Step One: Can you admit to yourself that you judge people on social media?

Step Two: Who are you judging the most on social media?

Step Three: What do they have that you want?

Step Four: What are they doing that you're not?

Step Five: How can you start doing this?

99% OF THE TIME, YOU JUDGE PEOPLE FOR "SELLING ALL THE TIME" , "ACTING DESPERATE FOR MONEY BY SELLING ALL THE TIME", "ONLY CARING ABOUT MONEY BY SELLING ALL THE TIME" , "EVERYTHING BEING A SALES PITCH"

AND SURPRISE, SURPRISE, IT MAKES YOU THE KIND OF PERSON THAT HAS TO PSYCHE THEMSELVES UP FOR A WEEK TO MAKE ONE SALES POST.

REPEAT AFTER MOI:

the more you sell, the more you sell

THAT'S RIGHT. THE MORE YOU SELL YOUR WARES, THE MORE YOU SELL YOUR WARES. FULL STOP. PERIOD.

I USUALLY RECOMMEND TO EVERYONE STRUGGLING WITH SALES TO FOLLOW KIM KARDASHIAN AND KYLIE JENNER, AND JUST SEE HOW MANY OF THEIR POSTS ARE SALES, AND HOW SELLING NON-STOP HAS NEVER HINDERED THEIR GROWTH WHATSOEVER. PEOPLE LOVE IT. THEY LOVE IT WHEN THEY DROP AN ENORMOUS PHOTO SHOOT, AND THEY LOVE IT WHEN THEY SHOW BTS ON STORIES. THEY LOVE THE NEW SKIMS DROP, THEY LOVE THE KYLIE SKIN, THEY LOVE IT ALL.

NOW, I KNOW THE KARDASHIANS ARE LOSING RELEVANCY AT THE MOMENT, BUT THEY'RE STILL A GREAT EXAMPLE OF BILLIONAIRE MATRIARCHS. AS THE COLLECTIVE MOVES INTO MATRIARCHY, IT'S IMPORTANT TO HAVE AN ARSENAL OF EXTREMELY WEALTHY MATRIARCH ROLE MODELS.

I'M NOT GOING TO SIT HERE AND CONVINCE YOU THAT MONEY IS GOOD. IF YOU'RE STILL AT THIS MONEY-HATING PHASE, THAT'S WHAT BREAKING BROKE 2.0 IS FOR. A POVERTY MINDSET NEVER GOES AWAY SPONTANEOUSLY OR ACCIDENTALLY. YOU HAVE TO BRAINWASH YOURSELF INTO A WEALTH MINDSET, WHICH TAKES 40 DAYS OF HARD WORK. 21 TO BECOME A NEW THINKER, AND AN ADDITIONAL 19 TO BECOME A NEW BEING. ALL MY WORKSHOPS ARE BUNDLED IN MY SCHOOL, SAFEHOUSE, AND WHEN YOU JOIN, WE TAKE AN INVENTORY OF YOUR LIFE AND I PERSONALLY PULL HOMEWORK FOR YOU BASED ON WHERE YOU ARE AND WHAT YOU NEED. MOST PEOPLE START WITH BREAKING BROKE 2.0

HERE'S WHAT YOU GET INSTEAD:

LIST OF FACTS ABOUT SPIRITUAL SELLING

People do not value what they don't pay for. If you don't sell your wares, either no one will value it, or no one will see it.

When you give away your work for free, the Universe gets the message that you do not see your gifts as valuable. As such, it is compelled to not pay you.

There are plenty of artists who never let anyone into their studio because they think people "won't get it". No matter what the artist says, they see people as idiots that don't get art, and that's a significant, ego-based block.

The art of sales is the art of solving a problem.

The art of launching is the art of serving first, and reaping the reward later.

Marketing and sales are natural when you are in touch with your value.

More money, more love, and more time are all blocked by low self worth.

The price is just the price. You don't need anyone's permission to set a price. (caveat: we do a whole module on pricing in Fuckless)

If you serve, you deserve.

You're only worried that you're being judged when you're judging others.

All wealth is a spiritual conspiracy.

When you discount your work because you think other people can't afford it, you are telling your client base you believe they will never succeed without charity. You are responsible for holding the unlimited beliefs for your clients. Not the limiting ones.

Other people will always say you're too expensive. That's their block. We are not building our businesses on other people's blocks.

Just because they're broke doesn't make your work cheap.

If you value yourself, your bank account shows it. If you do not value yourself, your bank account shows it. Take accountability for the inner state of your finances.

NOW THAT WE'VE WORKED THE SPIRITUAL, LET'S BRING IT INTO MARKETING

three levels of audiences:
this piece will help you understand exactly who you're marketing to in your audience.

THERE ARE THREE TYPES OF PEOPLE IN YOUR AUDIENCE. ONLY ONE OF THEM WILL BUY. YOU NEED TO COMMUNICATE WITH ALL THREE TYPES, AND EACH ONE SPEAKS A DIFFERENT LANGUAGE.

WE'RE GOING TO CALL THESE THREE TYPES COLD, WARM, AND HOT.

THE LANGUAGES THESE THREE TYPES SPEAK ARE VISION, PAIN, AND GAP.

THE VISION REPRESENTS WHERE THEY WANT TO BE.
THE PAIN REPRESENTS WHERE THEY ARE.
THE GAP REPRESENTS WHAT NEEDS TO BE DONE TO GO FROM PAIN TO VISION.

YOUR COLD CUSTOMERS MAKE UP THE MAJORITY OF YOUR SOCIAL MEDIA. THESE ARE THE BYSTANDERS, AS WELL AS THE REST OF YOUR CUSTOMER BASE. THE DIFFERENCE IS, THE COLD CUSTOMERS ARE JUST ON SOCIAL MEDIA. THEY ARE NEW TO FOLLOWING YOU, AND GETTING TO KNOW YOU. BASICALLY ANYTHING YOU SHARE ON SOCIAL MEDIA IS INDICATIVE OF THE VISION. YOU'RE DEMONSTRATING WHAT YOU KNOW, WHERE YOU ARE, AND WHERE YOU'VE BEEN. IDEALLY IN REGARDS TO YOUR PROFILE, AND LATER, MESSAGING. THE COLD AUDIENCE IS NOT READY TO MAKE A CHANGE JUST YET, THEY ARE STILL GETTING TO KNOW YOU.

TO COMMUNICATE WITH YOUR COLD AUDIENCE, JUST KEEP COMMUNICATING. WHATEVER YOU'RE PASSIONATE ABOUT, WHEN YOU'RE PASSIONATE ABOUT IT. USE YOUR DESIGN LIKE WE'VE BEEN WORKING HERE. WITH TIME, THE COLD WILL BECOME WARM.

The vision for the cold Fuckless customer is to be good at marketing...one day.

The biggest block is fear that other people will judge you for selling your unique gifts as much as you have judged others for selling theirs.

NEXT IS YOUR WARM CUSTOMERS. YOUR WARM CUSTOMERS ARE AWARE OF THE VISION, BUT THEY'RE NOT TOTALLY CLEAR ON THE PAIN. THEY'RE NOT TOTALLY CLEAR THAT THEY ARE IN PAIN. NOW, WHEN WE LEARN SALES TRIGGERS, YOU'LL LEARN THAT PEOPLE ARE MUCH MORE MOTIVATED BY PAIN THAN BY PLEASURE. THE WARM CUSTOMER JUST MIGHT BUY, BUT IN ORDER TO DO THAT, THEY NEED TO HEAR A LOT ABOUT THE PAIN.

The pain of the warm Fuckless customer is that they are constantly shushing themselves from doing what they want, and saying what they want. They know they have blocks around marketing, and they are slowly realizing no one is coming to save them. Their financial goals are so fucking old and unmet they're starting to think the Universe doesn't want that for them. Their marketing sometimes works and feels easy, and sometimes doesn't. They could be convinced at any time by any confident person that they're doing it "wrong" They're a slave for the approval of others, and they don't really know it. They're afraid of press unconsciously, though they want that recognition BAD.

What they need to hear a lot from me is the degree to which they are imprisoning themselves. That's the pain.

THE WARM CUSTOMERS ARE ON YOUR NEWSLETTER LIST, OR ANY MORE INTIMATE SETTING WHERE THEY CAN GET MORE FROM YOU. IF YOU DON'T HAVE A NEWSLETTER LIST, GO MAKE ONE IMMEDIATELY. FOR THE LAST 20 YEARS THE NEWSLETTER HAS DOMINATED ALL THE SALES FUNNELS, BECAUSE PEOPLE HAVE THEIR BUSINESS PANTS ON WHEN THEY CHECK EMAIL, AND THEIR SWEATPANTS ON WHEN THEY CHECK SOCIAL. THEY'RE READY TO BE SOLD TO IN EMAIL, AND THEY'RE NOT AS READY IN SOCIAL MEDIA. THEY'VE ALSO FOLLOWED YOU FROM ONE PLATFORM TO ANOTHER, THAT MAKES THEM WARM

The biggest block is fear that other people will judge you for selling your unique gifts as much as you have judged others for selling theirs.

finally, the HOT audience

THE HOT AUDIENCE IS BASICALLY SOLD. THEY MAY HAVE EVEN BOUGHT FROM YOU BEFORE. THEY'RE AWARE OF THE VISION, AND AWARE OF THE PAIN. THE HOT CUSTOMER IS THE ONE ON YOUR SALES PAGE, AND WHAT THEY NEED TO BE SOLD IS THE EXACT METHOD THAT YOU WILL BE USING TO BRIDGE THE GAP FOR THEM. THEY REALLY DON'T NEED A LOT OF CONVINCING EMAILS, AND YOU CAN SPARE YOURSELF ALL THAT NOISE BY JUST GIVING EACH CUSTOMER WHAT THEY WANT. THE METHOD.

THE HOT AUDIENCE ALSO HAS FAQ'S, SO YOU WOULD DO WELL TO ANSWER AND ELIMINATE ALL THE POSSIBLE DOWNSIDE RIGHT THERE ON THE SALES PAGE. ASK YOUR AUDIENCE! LIKE I'M ASKING YOU NOW.
DO YOU HAVE ANY QUESTIONS YOU NEED ANSWERED REGARDING THIS PROCESS? ANY CONCERNS HERE? REACH OUT AT SUPPORT@MAMIONAMI.COM

IT'S NEVER INCONVENIENT TO SOLVE A PROBLEM.

the exact Fuckless method:

50% INNER WORK: 50% OUTER WORK. NO MISTAKES.
45 MINUTES OF VIDEO CLASS EVERY WEEK FOR TEN WEEKS
GO AT YOUR OWN PACE.

INNER WORK:
BECOMING AUTHENTIC

KNOW
YOUR SELF

YOUR
POISE

SHOW
YOUR
SELF

Y

JR
TS

T
!

OUTER WORK:
AUTHENTIC MARKETING

MARKET

DATA

LAUNCHING

OFFER

MESS-
AGING

PRODUCT

CUSTOMER

YOUR LAUNCH
STRATEGY

PRODUCT
DEVELOPMENT

The biggest block is fear that other people will judge you for selling your unique gifts as much as you have judged others for selling theirs.

Let's recap the audiences:

Your social media wants the vision.
That's the cold audience.

The newsletter list wants the pain.
That's the warm audience.

The sales page wants the method for bridging the gap.
That's the hot audience.

Easy, right?

Okay so we've covered our inner work,
covered our outer work,
now we're ready for some human design.

The biggest block is fear that other people will judge you for selling your unique gifts as much as you have judged others for selling theirs.

Human Design: Lesson Three

Brand

Your brand:

When you have it your way, it just tastes better.

YOUR BRAND IS YOUR VIBE, YOUR BUSINESS'S MAIN VIBE. THIS IS YOUR FRONT OF HOUSE, BABY. THIS IS WHAT YOU ARE HERE TO SERVE. IF YOU LEAN INTO THIS PART OF YOUR NATURE, EVERYTHING ELSE WILL FLOW.
IF YOU'RE ALIGNED HERE, AND YOU KNOW WHAT IT MEANS *FOR YOU* TO BE IN ALIGNMENT AND OUT OF ALIGNMENT, YOU WILL BE ABLE TO WEATHER ALL MANNER OF SHITSTORMS. YOU WON'T CARE IF OTHER PEOPLE SAY IT'S "RIGHT" OR NOT. IT'S YOUR BRAND. IT'S ON BRAND FOR YOU.

go grab your chart. The big one.

YOUR BRAND IS YOUR CONSCIOUS SUN. UNLESS YOU ARE A REFLECTOR, IN WHICH CASE IT IS YOUR CONSCIOUS MOON.

THIS IS THE TOP **RIGHT** OF YOUR CHART.

WE SEE A NUMBER THERE, THAT'S THE GATE NUMBER, AND MY PERSONAL FAVORITE PLACE TO LOOK IT UP IS ON HUMANDESIGNSYSTEM.CO

I JUST TYPE IN "GATE _ _ _ _ _ _ HUMANDESIGNSYSTEM " INTO GOOGLE.

BEFORE WE FILL THIS IN ON YOUR HUMAN DESIGN PLANETS PAGE, LETS CLARIFY WHAT THIS BIG-ASS PIECE ACTUALLY MEANS FOR US.

The biggest block is fear that other people will judge you for selling your unique gifts as much as you have judged others for selling theirs.

Take that knowledge and make it your TRUTH, bitches!!!

What is my brand here to do?

What do I love about my brand?

How have I resisted this in myself?

When my brand is aligned it gives:

When my brand is out of alignment it gives:

Understanding my brand gives me the freedom to:

Understanding my brand gives me permission to:

Understanding my brand means I no longer have to:

Understanding my brand means I won't be tolerating:

Understanding my brand means I'm going to be on the lookout for:

I NOW CHOOSE TO:

NOW we can go fill in the gate number on your HD page.

The biggest block is fear that other people will judge you for selling your unique gifts as much as you have judged others for selling theirs.

Brand Case Studies:

NAME: Aubrey Plaza

GATE: 52 - Gate of Inaction

BRAND: Aubrey is all about the deadpan, it's what makes her unique. Gate 52 is often interpreted to be uncommunicative, inactive... deadpan, basically. This is SO on brand for her.

NAME: Azealia Banks

GATE: 20 - Gate of THE NOW

BRAND: Azealia has a reputation of going OFF. Like unhinged style. Out of nowhere, maxing out the stories. While others might say that's unprofessional, her brand is all about communicating the NOW and what she loves and hates in the NOW. On brand Azealia! You're my favorite female rapper.

The biggest block is fear that other people will judge you for selling your unique gifts as much as you have judged others for selling theirs.

Brand Case Studies:

NAME: Grimes

GATE: 36- Gate of Crisis

BRAND: I stan Grimes and will be forever devastated that her and Azealia's collab didn't happen. If you know about Grimes' obsessive nature when it comes to... everything. With gate 36 it goes crisis > coping > liberation. A new crisis, followed by obsessively dealing with it however you can , then a transformation, then a new crisis

NAME: Ye

GATE: 45 - Gate of THE KING

BRAND: This gate is also called the gate of the Gatherer, and it's about leading the community to material prosperity and well-being. They attract all the right people for this. Ye, however he does it, is always teaching about self-respect, and not allowing anyone, anywhere, to disrespect you.

I feel like he was really leaning into this brand with Donda U & other projects, but he did take a big not-self detour post 2020 so it got shaky. I think he'll come back hard because he's SO good at showing the collective what they want, as well as what level of self respect they NEED

The biggest block is fear that other people will judge you for selling your unique gifts as much as you have judged others for selling theirs.

Brand Case Studies:

NAME: Tony Robbins

GATE: 55 - Gate of Abundance

BRAND: I really wanted to use someone in my industry, and TR has been a longtime role model for me on spiritual wealth. He's worth 4B and made it all from being a GREAT man.

Surprise surprise, his brand is all about understanding that wealth is a spiritual equation. Period. His last two books on money changed my life, and were SO on brand.

NAME: ONAMI

GATE: 10 - Gate of the Self

BRAND: This gate is all about having a deep love for yourself (I mean... look at this face!) and an absolute NEED for authenticity. This gate impacts and inspires authenticity through a very natural and unaffected behavior.

when combined with my profile, I can be very real about what a difficult journey it was for me to become this way, and save you a lot of time.

am I on brand? Tell me in the chat!

The biggest block is fear that other people will judge you for selling your unique gifts as much as you have judged others for selling theirs.

I HAVE SO MANY LITTLE HACKS LIKE THIS FOR HUMAN DESIGN, AND SOME OTHER PIECES WE WILL LOOK AT DURING THE COURSE OF FUCKLESS ARE:

YOUR MESSAGING, YOUR COMPANY CULTURE, YOUR BRAND'S NEEDS, YOUR MONEY MAKING POTENTIAL, YOUR MONEY BLOCK, YOUR INCARNATION'S CROSS TO BEAR, SHOULD YOU BE THE FACE OF YOUR BUSINESS OR NOT, YOUR PERSONAL MOTIVATION STYLE, COLLABORATIONS, AND EVEN DIET.

 I WANT SO BAD TO DROP THEM ALL RIGHT HERE AND NOW, AND IT TOOK A LOT OF PLANNING TO FIGURE OUT EXACTLY WHAT PLACEMENTS EACH PIECE WOULD GO IN SO THAT THE WORK CAN BE INTEGRATED. AS FUN AS IT IS TO HEAR ALL THE TRICKS, IF YOU DON'T KNOW HOW TO APPLY THEM IT'S ONLY FUN FOR THE DAY THAT YOU GET THE INFORMATION. IT'S NOT APPLICABLE.

it's time to make a decision.

YOU HAVE STARTED THE BALL ROLLING HERE, BUT YOU CAN DROP THE MOMENTUM AS EASILY AS YOU PICKED IT UP. **EVERY INDIVIDUAL HAS A DIFFERENT AUTHORITY, WHICH MEANS WE ALL MAKE DECISIONS DIFFERENTLY.** THIS WORKSHOP IS NOT ALWAYS AVAILABLE, **AND WHEN IT IS, YOU NEED TO JUMP ON IT. THERE IS A FIVE DAY FREE TRIAL, SO YOU CAN GET STARTED ON MODULE ONE FOR $0, BUT IT IS A MAGICAL PROCESS AND CADENCE IS IMPORTANT. YOU WANT TO SHOW UP AND HIT IT CONSISTENTLY, KEEPING A NICE STRONG PACE.** IT'S TIME TO SHIFT THIS CONVERSATION TO HUMAN DESIGN, BECAUSE WE ALL MAKE DECISIONS DIFFERENTLY, AND OUR INTUITION SOUNDS DIFFERENT FOR EACH AND EVERY ONE OF US. **THIS IS YOUR AUTHORITY. YOUR AUTHORITY AND YOUR STRATEGY ARE CONSIDERED TO BE YOUR TWO MOST IMPORTANT ASPECTS OF HUMAN DESIGN. MASTER THESE TWO, YOU MASTER ALL**

Human Design: Lesson Four

Authority and decision making

Your authority.

THE AUTHORITY TYPES ARE CONNECTED TO YOUR DEFINED CENTERS AND ASSOCIATED WITH YOUR TYPE. **MOST HUMAN DESIGN CHART SOFTWARE LIST YOUR AUTHORITY OUT IN A CLEAR WAY – GENETIC MATRIX LUMPS IT IN WITH YOUR TYPE, SO IF YOU'RE AN EMOTIONAL MANIFESTOR, THE EMOTIONAL PART IS YOUR AUTHORITY.** GO PEEP YOUR CHART AND HAVE IT ON HAND.

If you are a Generator or MG

IF YOU ARE A GENERATOR, YOU HAVE SACRAL AUTHORITY UNLESS OTHERWISE SPECIFIED. THAT MEANS THAT YOUR FIRST REACTION TO THE FOLLOWING QUESTIONS WILL EITHER BE A HELL YES OR A HELL NO, OR A SOUND. IF YOU NEED MORE INFORMATION, YOU CAN ASK IN THE FUCKLESS QA ON THE FREE VERSION OF OUR APP.

DO YOU WANT TO TAKE THIS COURSE?

DO YOU WANT TO GET BETTER AT MARKETING?

DOES A SERIES OF SHORT VIDEOS AND WORKSHEETS SOUND GOOD TO YOU?

DO YOU HAVE SPACE TO TAKE A 30 MINUTE PER WEEK WORKSHOP?

IS AUTHENTICITY AND MARKETING A PRIORITY FOR YOU RIGHT NOW?

DOES IT FEEL LIKE THIS IS WHAT YOU'VE BEEN WAITING FOR?

<u>IF ITS A YES, GO GET YOUR FREE TRIAL RIGHT NOW</u>. GENNIES GET STUPID WHEN THEY PROCRASTINATE. YOU DO NOT WANT TO MISS Q&A. NO DEADLINE. ACT NOW AND KEEP YOUR PACE. DO NOT LOSE MOMENTUM PERIOD. YOU ARE FIRST IN LINE, ALWAYS, AND EVERY OTHER TYPE IS SO JEALOUS YOU CAN DO THAT.

if you have emotional authority:

YOU DON'T KNOW RIGHT AWAY, SO GIVE YOURSELF A 14 DAY DEADLINE TO DECIDE AND HONOR IT. UNDERSTAND THAT YOUR WAVE CHANGES SO WHAT SEEMS LIKE A GREAT IDEA IN ONE MOMENT WILL SOUND LIKE A TERRIBLE IDEA THE NEXT, AND THEN SOUND LIKE A GREAT IDEA AGAIN. MAKE A PROS AND CONS LIST, AND HONOR THAT DEADLINE. DISHONORING YOUR DEADLINES IS WHAT MAKES YOU UNSUCCESSFUL.

if you have a self-projected authority:

IF YOU HAVE A SELF-PROJECTED AUTHORITY, YOU NEED TO TALK IT OUT WITH SOMEONE TO BE CLEAR. THAT SOMEONE SHOULD NOT BE ME, BUT IT COULD BE SOCIAL MEDIA. YOU CAN ALSO TALK IT OUT IN FEELINGS ROOM. YOU DON'T NEED OTHER PEOPLE'S INPUT, JUST OTHER PEOPLE'S WITNESS. GIVE YOURSELF A ONE WEEK DEADLINE AND HONOR IT.

if you have splenic authority:

IF YOU HAVE SPLENIC AUTHORITY, IT'S A STILL, SMALL VOICE THAT IS GUIDING YOU WITH NO CONTEXT WHATSOEVER. YOU HAVE THE ANSWER RIGHT NOW, LIKE THE SACRAL AUTHORITY, SO YOU CAN DECIDE RIGHT AWAY. PROCRASTINATING KILLS THE SPLEEN. MOVE NOW. ACT NOW. YOU CAN USE THESE QUESTIONS TO TAP IN:

DOES TAKING FUCKLESS RIGHT NOW SEEM HARD OR SOFT? SOFT IS YES.
DOES TAKING FUCKLESS RIGHT NOW SEEM OPEN OR CLOSED? OPEN IS YES.
DOES TAKING FUCKLESS RIGHT NOW SEEM EASY OR HARD? EASY IS RIGHT.

if you have mental authority:

YOU NEED TO TALK IT OUT WITH PEOPLE OR IN YOUR JOURNAL. MAKE A PROS AND CONS LIST, AND BE DONE WITH IT IN ONE SESSION, DON'T KEEP IT GOING. YOU NEED TO HEAR ALL SIDES OF IT TO BE CERTAIN, SO GIVE YOURSELF THAT SPACE. PROS AND CONS ARE WHAT THE MIND IS GREAT FOR. ACT IMMEDIATELY AFTER YOUR SESSION SO THAT THE MIND DOESN'T VEER INTO NOT-SELF. YOU HAVE TO HONOR THE ANSWER BY NOT ASKING AGAIN.

if you have ego aka heart authority:

IT'S A FEELING THING. USE THESE QUESTIONS TO CLARIFY, AND YOU HAVE A ONE WEEK DEADLINE.

DOES FUCKLESS FEEL EXCITING TO YOU?
DOES FUCKLESS FEEL FUN TO YOU?
IS THIS SOMETHING YOU WANT TO DO?
HOW DOES IT FEEL TO MOVE TOWARDS THIS?
HOW DOES IT FEEL TO MOVE AWAY FROM THIS?

if you have lunar authority:

IF YOU'RE A REFLECTOR AND DON'T KNOW ME, SET A TIMER FOR ONE 28 DAY LUNAR CYCLE FROM TODAY, AND DON'T LET ANYONE PRESSURE YOU INTO MAKING A DECISION FASTER THAN THAT. DURING THE LUNAR CYCLE, THINK ABOUT WHAT YOU REALLY WANT AND WHAT IT IS GOING TO TAKE TO GET THERE. I ALSO RECOMMEND NOT TAKING THE WHOLE COMMUNITY ON, IT'S NOT YOUR RESPONSIBILITY TO KEEP THE COMMUNITY MOVING. YOU CAN JUST RECEIVE HERE.

IF YOU ALREADY KNOW ME, REFLECT ON IF YOU SEE ME AS AN AUTHORITY HERE OR NOT. BECAUSE OF YOUR TIMING YOU MIGHT MISS THE FIRST QA, BUT YOU WON'T MISS THE SECOND ONE.

THAT BIT ABOUT YOUR BRAND BEING YOUR CONSCIOUS MOON, MOST HD PEOPLE DON'T KNOW THIS, AND WOULD TELL YOU ITS THE SUN. THAT IS NOT CORRECT. I DO NOT FORGET ABOUT REFLECTORS, AND I SPEAK THE LANGUAGE.

121

TO ENROLL IN FUCKLESS ALL YOU NEED IS AN ACTIVE SAFEHOUSE SUBSCRIPTION, WHICH GETS YOU ACCESS TO EVERY OTHER WORKSHOP AS WELL.

MAMIONAMI.COM/SAFEHOUSE IS ALL YOU NEED.

GO AHEAD AND COLOR IN ALL THE CENTERS
YOU HAVE FILLED IN ON YOUR HUMAN
DESIGN CHART, AND CIRCLE WHICH CENTER
IS YOUR AUTHORITY.

reviews from last round:

I have made so many up levels since working w @ONAMI - expanded my brick and mortar business increasing my passive income etc and now I am **finally** feeling even more confident everyday that I Do have So Much More to offer than my hands !! And it feels good

All that I Am has been a Long Time Coming & I Am Becoming All that I Am 🖤

@ONAMI I just read the letter to your mother in law and it was sooo good & affirming for me

One of the friendships I lost during Fuckless was due to me "changing my mind so much I give her whiplash" (among other shit but that was like her last fuck you to me) and although I am not a 6/3 I am a 1/3 !! So much change like coins in the hunnnndreds !! I've always been this way and I have lost friendships to it before now that I think about it .

Anyway just wanted to say thanks
May have been for Magics mama but it landed for me too xox

Posted in #chat | Aug 10th, 2022 at 11:52 AM

reviews from last round:

F*ckless has made my world almost unrecognizable.. In the best way possible! Things have begun to effortlessly click into place.. the synchronicities are profound.. like cogs finally fitting into the proper groove.. There are these incredible times of being very liberated & in step w/who I am supposed to be.. There are still some uneasy moments.. The difference is now I have the tools & clarity to handle myself w/grace as I move forward grateful for all life gives me. Less judgment for both myself & others has naturally occurred as I find my very own authentic flow. Which for me means forgiving myself & understanding my truth has worth w/out lies or embellishment. I hear more as I speak less. The lessons I learned in F*ckless are absolutely priceless. It was these gems of knowledge that has allowed me to shine brighter than I believed possible.. Sending Love & Appreciation to you dear Onami..
💙TY💙

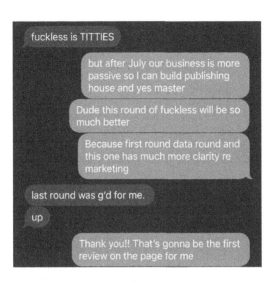

fuckless is TITTIES

but after July our business is more passive so I can build publishing house and yes master

Dude this round of fuckless will be so much better

Because first round data round and this one has much more clarity re marketing

last round was g'd for me.

up

Thank you!! That's gonna be the first review on the page for me

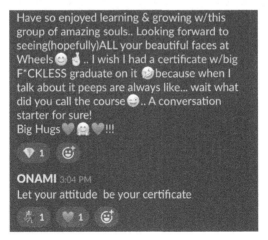

Have so enjoyed learning & growing w/this group of amazing souls.. Looking forward to seeing(hopefully)ALL your beautiful faces at Wheels 😊 ✌️.. I wish I had a certificate w/big F*CKLESS graduate on it 😂 because when I talk about it peeps are always like... wait what did you call the course 😅.. A conversation starter for sure!
Big Hugs 💜 👻 💜!!!

💎 1   😊⁺

ONAMI 3:04 PM
Let your attitude be your certificate

🏃 1   ❤️ 1   😊⁺

reviews from last round:

Thank you for such a good call yesterday ladies - I seriously felt such a supportive pouring in of love from each and every one of you !!

The more I step into my truth the more I have been processing deep grief that I know I've been holding for eons! Releasing so much, moving so much and crying so much! For every time I betrayed myself ! Stayed when I should have gone! Said yes when I meant no!

All that I Am has been a Long Time Coming & I Am Becoming All that I Am 🤍

I love you all very much 🤍

reviews from last round:

I guess that's obvious to me now..
My body/brain has gone thru soo soo
many changes since F*cklss..
Off BP pharmaceuticals to beets/nitric
oxide a WiN.. My 40 day sacrifice is
wrapping up this Sat on ♏ .. TY so
very much for all you share.. I find
myself constantly learning so much
from you!!! It's like I'm standing in such
a better place in life.. Personally I think
w/o having done F*ckless 1st .. Wheels
would not be making the glorious yet
painful at times impact.. TY for doing
the heavy lifting & allowing others to
learn from your experiences. I admire
your ability to tell it like it is mistakes &
successes..
You are so very loved & appreciated my
dear 💜 🌷

❤️

THE REST OF THIS BOOK IS INTENDED FOR USE WITH THE ONLINE WORKSHOP, FUCKLESS.

YOU WON'T UNDERSTAND HOW TO DO THE WORKBOOK WITHOUT HEARING THE LESSONS AND KNOWING WHAT YOU'RE DOING ON PAPER.

Marketing Lessons are in the video workshop only.

PICK UP A FIVE DAY TRIAL OF THE WORKSHOP AT MAMIONAMI.COM/FUCKLESS

am I doing this for approval?

The function of this is to wake you up.
Please refer to the Orientation: LSD
and the Psych Ward video on your
dashboard. Thank you.

When was the last time you caught yourself doing something for approval?

Whose approval did you want?

Did you get it?

Why is this person's approval meaningful to you?

Are they experts in a field you would like to be an expert in?

Who's approval did you seek more as a child, your mother's or your father's?

Who did you have to be to get approval from them?

Whose approval would you most like today?

What would they say?

"let's have a moment of silence….."

that was a moment of silence for your insecurity. Cause we're about to annhilate that motherfucker."

draw a tombstone for your insecurity.

what makes you insecure?
immediately stop.

make a running list of things that make you insecure.
Talk about it in Fuckless chat if you need help!

NEWSLETTER: 1/26/22

I had recently discovered I was insecure.

I had been suspicious that my judgement wasn't my style, and that even though it's my human design, it doesn't work for me. Anyways it took me like six months of sifting until a former teacher (of course) wrote a post on insecurity and I recognized the taste.
I thought it was jealousy, which would create judgment , an infection of the Vissuda but it was actually a constant need for superiority (ahem) which is insecurity.

Diagnosing this took years and those of you who follow me know when I teach jealousy I always reference these accounts like, why can I not stop stalking them? Am I jealous? And I wasn't. I wasn't envying something they had and believing I wouldn't get it. I was insecure that I'd never be as good as them, and that's what's changing.

So insecurity is like carbonated water and it's insecure because it's unstable, and it's unstable because the base is loose, like a table. That's your muladhara . You feel like you don't belong, and if you don't belong you don't deserve. Because it's the root it really is related to stabilizing the income. It's what needs to happen FIRST.

Confidence is like crystal clear, cool water in a large fish tank. Like Blippi sink or swim, moms. Not a space, a gap, or a compromise when it comes to taking up and owning your space in the world. I need total confidence for this next round. The final frontier of *this round* of transformation. I can't afford to be insecure.

So what makes YOU insecure? Stop right now and think about it. Those teachers accounts hit different when you aren't insecure! You see yourself as one of them, as part of the wave that's bringing you all up together.

Can you handle that? How quickly will you use insecurity to cope with the fact that you are here HUNNY. It's your time. What makes you insecure? Stop now.

AN ENDLESS
NEED FOR
SUPERIORITY,
JUDGMENT OF
OTHERS, AND
PERFECTION IS
JUST EVIDENCE
OF ONE'S
INSECURITY

BIET SIMKIN

A MASK WORN
WHEN THE FACE HAS GROWN
BECOMES A WALL
THAT RUBS AND CUTS

RUMI

the function of this lesson is to get an idea of how often you are being authentic by getting an idea of how often you are being inauthentic. the sizzle is real.

Please refer to the Week One, Lying video before proceeding with the worksheet.

is it true?

the homework is simple.
but it ain't easy.

try not to lie for one week.

no embellishments,
white lies,
other people's stories,
or outright lies.

Observe.

To be transformed, the whole basis of your thoughts must change. But your thoughts cannot change unless you have new ideas, for you think from your ideas.

All transformation begins with an intense, burning desire to be transformed.

NEVILLE GODDARD

What is a story you always tell that isn't yours?

Why do you tell it?

How is it received when you tell it?

Whose story is it?

What do they have that you want?

Will any amount of telling their story get you what you want of theirs?

When was the last time you caught yourself embellishing a story?

Why do you think the story isn't strong enough without embellishments?

What truth are you not wanting to accept about your story when you embellish it?

What is the problem with sharing the story truthfully?

tell me your story, unfiltered.

know yourself.

The function of this lesson is to show you who you really are.
Please listen to Point One video on your dashboard before
filling out the worksheet.

This is one of the most powerful coaching tools, and when I did 1:1 still, every client would get this at some point. I call this the Identity Game.

We have so many stories about who we think we are. We have a outer self that we manicure and curate and present to the world (just look at social media), and often times it conflicts with the inner self that we show to no one. The excess of the outer story e.g. "I'm enormously successful" and the pressure of maintaining it can cause the inner self to create a self story that is at a major deficit, e.g. "I'm a complete failure.". Neither the story of being a success, or a failure is true. The inner self and the outer self are not aligned, this is the substance of what we call an identity crisis.

Please do this exercise with a pen and a paper. Don't just think it, please do it. I cannot possibly stress the potency of it.

Make a list of the aspects of your outer self. The side of you you present to the world, for example: brave, successful, calm, hopeful

Next to it please make another list, this time the aspects of your inner personality. You may notice some opposites arise, for example: worried, discouraged, frantic. More importantly you will notice some consistencies, for example: Outer Self - brave, Inner Self - brave.

Now please go through the list, and cross off every single aspect that is not a match on both sides. If it's not a match between the inner self and the outer self, it is not really you. They are just excess details that result in confusion, striving, and an identity crisis. Toss all these ideas of self into the garbage.

The ones that remain, that are congruent with the inner and outer self; live from these aspects. If there are congruent aspects on both sides that you aren't happy with, e.g. worried, make those a priority for healing.
The rest, write down and put somewhere you can see them every day. Live your life from these aspects. Identify with these aspects. Be proud of them. By ridding ourselves of what we are not, we can relax into the nature of who we are. An added bonus is you never have to worry about maintaining what you're presenting. You can finally just be.

the identity game

inner self   outer self

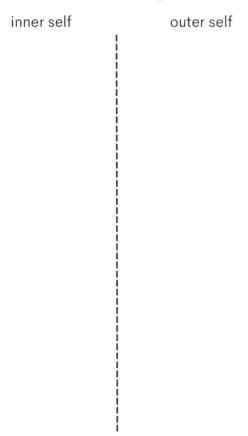

LIVE FROM THESE ASPECTS:

the function of this is to convince you that:

my flaws are my gifts
my flaws are my gifts
my flaws are my gifts
my flaws are my gifts
my flaws are my gifts
my flaws are my gifts
my flaws are my gifts
my flaws are my gifts
my flaws are my gifts
my flaws are my gifts
my flaws are my gifts
my flaws are my gifts
my flaws are my gifts
my flaws are my gifts
my flaws are my gifts
my flaws are my gifts
my flaws are my gifts
my flaws are my gifts

please refer to the Point Two: Flaws video on your dashboard

"I managed to succeed in spite of my:

"I am talented even though I have:

"Everything is good about me except my:

"As a kid I was always told to:

"As a child I was punished for:

"Even now I'm still afraid to:

"People like me as long as I don't:

"I just feel like no one would want me if:

"The perfect version of me just needs:"

It is our light, not our darkness that most frightens us. Your playing small does not serve the world. There is nothing enlightened about shrinking so that other people won't feel insecure around you

MARIANNE WILLIAMSON

becoming bulletproof.

POINT THREE: LIMITATIONS

The function of this lesson is to disarm your critics before they can strike. Please refer to the Point Four: Limitations video on your dashboard.

write an amazing headline about yourself, and where it's featured too.

write a not so amazing headline about yourself, and where it's featured too.

Who specifically are you afraid will reject you if you come forward in your fullness?

What specifically do you think they'll say?

How are you saying this to yourself?

How can you shift this disempowering internal monologue to one that uplifts and empowers you?

What are the three best things someone could call you?

How can you see this as true?

What are the three worst things someone could call you?

How are these things true?

Who are the three best people you could be compared to and why?

How is this comparison true?

Who are the three worst people you could be compared to and why?

How are these comparisons true? (Don't be lazy.)

the ritual.

The importance of this module is not to be underestimated.
FOR REAL. This has been tested and proven.
This is mathematical magic and this is the point where ,by law,
you will fall off course.
Work HARD here. Do more than you're commanded to.

please refer to Point Three: The Ritual on your dashboard.

things I said I'd do and never did:

you will now adopt a forty day ritual.

this is not a joke. do not miss one day.
this has been tested.

your ritual should be daily, and it should be either action
towards one of the goals you said you would like to
accomplish e.g. writing that book daily, reading 30
minutes daily, running incrementally towards a 5k goal,
selling every day, immaculate AM/PM routine, yoga,
meditation, or breathwork every day.

OR

you can develop a routine that feels doable to you and
stick to it.

your results are a reward from your efforts. Don't be lazy.

for forty days I will:

for forty days I will not:

my forty days begins on:

my forty days ends on:

sign:

_____

(and be grateful I'm not making you sign it in blood)

FILL OUT EVERY SINGLE ONE

BECAUSE I TRUST MYSELF I:

BECAUSE I TRUST MYSELF I:

BECAUSE I TRUST MYSELF I:

BECAUSE I TRUST MYSELF I:

BECAUSE I TRUST MYSELF I:

BECAUSE I TRUST MYSELF I:

BECAUSE I TRUST MYSELF I:

BECAUSE I TRUST MYSELF I:

BECAUSE I TRUST MYSELF I:

BECAUSE I TRUST MYSELF I:

BECAUSE I TRUST MYSELF I:

BECAUSE I TRUST MYSELF I:

BECAUSE I TRUST MYSELF I:

BECAUSE I TRUST MYSELF I:

autobiography in five chapters

by Portia Nelson

I

I walk down the street.
There is a deep hole in the sidewalk
I fall in.
I am lost...
I am hopeless.
It isn't my fault.
It takes forever to find a way out.

II

I walk down the same street.
There is a deep hole in the sidewalk.
I pretend I don't see it.
I fall in again.
I can't believe I'm in the same place.
But it isn't my fault.
It still takes a long time to get out.

III

I walk down the same street.
There is a deep hole in the sidewalk.
I see it is there.
I still fall in...it's a habit
My eyes are open; I know where I am;
It is my fault.
I get out immediately.

IV

I walk down the same street.
There is a deep hole in the sidewalk.
I walk around it.

V

I walk down another street.

creativity has four seasons:

SPRING - follicular- wands- new ideas

SUMMER- ovulation - cups - networking

FALL- luteal - pentacles - hunker down
and get it done

WINTER - menstrual - swords- rest

what season are you in?

what do you know you need. having been here before?

WHEREVER WE THINK WE NEED MORE SELF-DISCIPLINE WE ACTUALLY NEED MORE SELF-LOVE.

TARA MOHR

your story.

these three Painkillers will help you to sift your message from the mess. I recommend addressing these to:

1.) child you
2.) the parent whose approval you craved more
3.) a time that was particularly challenging for you, e.g. "2020"

You're meant to tell the emotional truth here, even if you're the only one that sees it this way.

you have two more of these in the back, you can get more in my book Painkillers, 55 sheets.

Painkiller (one sheet)

an ONAMI initiative

Date: _____ Name: _____

Step One: The Emotional Truth

DISCLAIMER: This worksheet is yours and trust me, you don't want anyone else to read it. This worksheet contains the emotional truth. You don't need to fact-check yourself, be exact, or even make sense. This may or may not be emotional for you.

Are you willing to tell the emotional truth here, even if you're the only one who sees the story this way?

☐ Willing ☐ Open ☐ Unsure ☐ Unwilling

Step Two: Diagnosing Grief

Conflicting feelings occur when a great change results in unfinished business. Some examples of a great change would be: loss of a job, moving, breaking up with someone, a change in routine, or the birth of a child.

Have you recently experienced a great change?
☐ Yes ☐ No ☐ Not Sure

Unfinished business is things you wish you did **differently, better, or more.** Do you feel like you have unfinished business with something or someone?
☐ Yes ☐ No ☐ Not Sure

Unfinished business creates painful energetic cords that make it hard for us to "forgive & forget". Unfinished business may feel like reaching for something or someone that was always there only to find out that when you need it one last time, it's still not there. Unfinished business may also feel like, reaching for something or someone who was never there, only to find out when you need it one last time, it's still not there.

Are you having a hard time forgiving and forgetting something or someone who was **always** there?
☐ Yes ☐ No ☐ Not Sure

Are you having a hard time forgiving and forgetting something or someone who was **never** there?
☐ Yes ☐ No ☐ Not Sure

Step Three: Completion Letter

In writing the completion letter, you will be closing the unfinished business causing you optional pain. You are not saying goodbye to the person, place, or thing, only the pain. There is no need to contact the person, living, dead, or unborn for healing to occur. There is no need to tell anyone you've forgiven them. You will be saying goodbye to the pain.

Are you ready to begin? ☐ Yes ☐ No ☐ Not Sure
Initial here: _____ Thank you.

Please write the name of the person, place or thing you are grieving.

Dear _____, I've been reviewing our relationship and there are some things I need to say.

My first memory with you is: _____

When I revisit this memory, I must acknowledge that: _____

Initial here: _____ Thank you.

Dear _____ as I continue this journey towards completing our story, I need to acknowledge that in all relationships there are ups and downs. I need to acknowledge that in our relationship, there were ups and downs. In order to heal, I need to honor these stories with no criticism, analysis, or judgment. This may or may not be emotional. But I will not skip any.
Initial _____ Thank you.

_____, the first high point in our relationship that comes to mind is: _____

When I remember this I: (select one)
☐ Need to apologize ☐ Need to forgive ☐ Need to honor that _____

Initial here: _____ Thank you.

Dear _____, I now need to acknowledge a low point to heal from these painful cords that have bound us in pain for so long. The first low point coming to mind is:_____

_____

When I remember this I: (select one) ☐ Need to apologize ☐ Need to forgive ☐ Need to honor that_____

_____

Initial here: _____ Thank you.

Dear _____, there are only two more high points and two more low points to recall and then I will be free from the pain that binds us. The second high point that comes to mind is:_____

_____

When I remember this I: (select one) ☐ Need to apologize ☐ Need to forgive ☐ Need to honor that_____

_____

The second low point that comes to mind is: _____

_____

When I remember this I: (select one) ☐ Need to apologize ☐ Need to forgive ☐ Need to honor that_____

_____

Initial here: _____ Thank you.

Dear _____, the final high point I need to review is:_____

_____

When I remember this I: (select one) ☐ Need to apologize ☐ Need to forgive ☐ Need to honor that_____

_____

Dear _____, the final low point I need to acknowledge is:_____

_____

When I remember this I: (select one) ☐ Need to apologize ☐ Need to forgive ☐ Need to honor that_____

_____

Initial here: _____ Thank you.

Dear _____, I've learned so much from reviewing our relationship.

In order to be done here once and for all and remove all blocks from receiving, I need to acknowledge that if I had known we were really saying goodbye there is at least one thing I wish I would have done differently and that thing is:_____

_____

Initial _____ Thank you.

And if I had known we were really saying goodbye there is at least one thing I wish I would have done better. That thing is: _____

Initial _____ Thank you.

Finally, _____, I need to acknowledge that in order to heal there is at least one thing I wish I would have done more, and that thing is: _____

Initial _____ Thank you.

Now, _____ the time has come for me to say goodbye, because when something is LEAVING, and the pain attached to this name I write IS leaving, you say goodbye. Not see you later. Goodbye. I will now make my closing statement.
Just because _____,
doesn't mean_____
_____, when I write "GOODBYE" next to your name, the process will be completed. All barriers to receiving caused by the grief of this relationship will also be removed. When you are ready please write "GOODBYE Name" below:

_____

Initial _____ Thank you.

Painkiller (one sheet)

an ONAMI initiative

Date: _____ Name: _____

Step One: The Emotional Truth

DISCLAIMER: This worksheet is yours and trust me, you don't want anyone else to read it. This worksheet contains the emotional truth. You don't need to fact-check yourself, be exact, or even make sense. This may or may not be emotional for you.

Are you willing to tell the emotional truth here, even if you're the only one who sees the story this way?

☐ Willing ☐ Open ☐ Unsure ☐ Unwilling

Step Two: Diagnosing Grief

Conflicting feelings occur when a great change results in unfinished business. Some examples of a great change would be: loss of a job, moving, breaking up with someone, a change in routine, or the birth of a child.

Have you recently experienced a great change?
☐ Yes ☐ No ☐ Not Sure

> Unfinished business is things you wish you did **differently, better, or more.** Do you feel like you have unfinished business with something or someone?
> ☐ Yes ☐ No ☐ Not Sure

Unfinished business creates painful energetic cords that make it hard for us to "forgive & forget". Unfinished business may feel like reaching for something or someone that was always there only to find out that when you need it one last time, it's still not there. Unfinished business may also feel like, reaching for something or someone who was never there, only to find out you need it one last time, it's still not there.

> Are you having a hard time forgiving and forgetting something or someone who was **always** there?
> ☐ Yes ☐ No ☐ Not Sure

> Are you having a hard time forgiving and forgetting something or someone who was **never** there?
> ☐ Yes ☐ No ☐ Not Sure

Step Three: Completion Letter

In writing the completion letter, you will be closing the unfinished business causing you optional pain. You are not saying goodbye to the person, place, or thing, only the pain. There is no need to contact the person, living, dead, or unborn for healing to occur. There is no need to tell anyone you've forgiven them. You will be saying goodbye to the pain.

> Are you ready to begin? ☐ Yes ☐ No ☐ Not Sure
> Initial here: _____ Thank you.

> Please write the name of the person, place or thing you are grieving.
>
> Dear _____, I've been reviewing our relationship and there are some things I need to say.
>
> My first memory with you is: _____
> _____
>
> When I revisit this memory, I must acknowledge that:_____
> _____
>
> Initial here: _____ Thank you.

> Dear _____ as I continue this journey towards completing our story, I need to acknowledge that in all relationships there are ups and downs. I need to acknowledge that in our relationship, there were ups and downs. In order to heal, I need to honor these stories with no criticism, analysis, or judgment. This may or may not be emotional. But I will not skip any.
> Initial _____ Thank you.
>
> _____, the first high point in our relationship that comes to mind is:_____
> _____
>
> When I remember this I: (select one)
> ☐ Need to apologize ☐ Need to forgive ☐ Need to honor that_____
> _____
>
> Initial here: _____ Thank you.

Dear _____, I now need to acknowledge a low point to heal from these painful cords that have bound us in pain for so long. The first low point coming to mind is:_____

_____

When I remember this I: (select one) ☐ Need to apologize ☐ Need to forgive ☐ Need to honor that_____

_____

Initial here: _____ Thank you.

Dear _____, there are only two more high points and two more low points to recall and then I will be free from the pain that binds us. The second high point that comes to mind is: _____

_____

When I remember this I: (select one) ☐ Need to apologize ☐ Need to forgive ☐ Need to honor that_____

_____

The second low point that comes to mind is: _____

_____

When I remember this I: (select one) ☐ Need to apologize ☐ Need to forgive ☐ Need to honor that_____

_____

Initial here: _____ Thank you.

Dear _____, the final high point I need to review is:_____

_____

When I remember this I: (select one) ☐ Need to apologize ☐ Need to forgive ☐ Need to honor that_____

_____

Dear _____, the final low point I need to acknowledge is:_____

_____

When I remember this I: (select one) ☐ Need to apologize ☐ Need to forgive ☐ Need to honor that_____

_____

Initial here: _____ Thank you.

Dear _____, I've learned so much from reviewing our relationship.

In order to be done here once and for all and remove all blocks from receiving, I need to acknowledge that if I had known we were really saying goodbye there is at least one thing I wish I would have done differently and that thing is:_____

_____

Initial _____ Thank you.

And if I had known we were really saying goodbye there is at least one thing I wish I would have done better.
That thing is: _____

Initial _____ Thank you.

Finally, _____, I need to acknowledge that in order to heal there is at least one thing I wish I would have done more, and that thing is:_____

Initial _____ Thank you.

Now, _____ the time has come for me to say goodbye, because when something is LEAVING, and the pain attached to this name I write IS leaving, you say goodbye. Not see you later. Goodbye. I will now make my closing statement.
Just because _____,

doesn't mean_____
_____, when I write "GOODBYE" next to your name, the process will be completed. All barriers to receiving caused by the grief of this relationship will also be removed. When you are ready please write "GOODBYE Name" below:

_____

Initial _____ Thank you.

Painkiller (one sheet)

an ONAMI initiative

Date: _____ Name: _____

Step One: The Emotional Truth

DISCLAIMER: This worksheet is yours and trust me, you don't want anyone else to read it. This worksheet contains the emotional truth. You don't need to fact-check yourself, be exact, or even make sense. This may or may not be emotional for you.

Are you willing to tell the emotional truth here, even if you're the only one who sees the story this way?

☐ Willing ☐ Open ☐ Unsure ☐ Unwilling

Step Two: Diagnosing Grief

Conflicting feelings occur when a great change results in unfinished business. Some examples of a great change would be: loss of a job, moving, breaking up with someone, a change in routine, or the birth of a child.

Have you recently experienced a great change?
☐ Yes ☐ No ☐ Not Sure

> Unfinished business is things you wish you did **differently, better, or more.** Do you feel like you have unfinished business with something or someone?
> ☐ Yes ☐ No ☐ Not Sure

Unfinished business creates painful energetic cords that make it hard for us to "forgive & forget". Unfinished business may feel like reaching for something or someone that was always there only to find out that when you need it one last time, it's still not there. Unfinished business may also feel like, reaching for something or someone who was never there, only to find out when you need it one last time, it's still not there.

> Are you having a hard time forgiving and forgetting something or someone who was **always** there?
> ☐ Yes ☐ No ☐ Not Sure

> Are you having a hard time forgiving and forgetting something or someone who was **never** there?
> ☐ Yes ☐ No ☐ Not Sure

Step Three: Completion Letter

In writing the completion letter, you will be closing the unfinished business causing you optional pain. You are not saying goodbye to the person, place, or thing, only the pain. There is no need to contact the person, living, dead, or unborn for healing to occur. There is no need to tell anyone you've forgiven them. You will be saying goodbye to the pain.

> Are you ready to begin? ☐ Yes ☐ No ☐ Not Sure
> Initial here: _____ Thank you.

> Please write the name of the person, place or thing you are grieving.
>
> Dear _____, I've been reviewing our relationship and there are some things I need to say.
>
> My first memory with you is: _____
> _____
>
> When I revisit this memory, I must acknowledge that:_____
> _____
>
> Initial here: _____ Thank you.

> Dear _____ as I continue this journey towards completing our story, I need to acknowledge that in all relationships there are ups and downs. I need to acknowledge that in our relationship, there were ups and downs. In order to heal, I need to honor these stories with no criticism, analysis, or judgment. This may or may not be emotional. But I will not skip any.
> Initial _____ Thank you.
>
> _____, the first high point in our relationship that comes to mind is:_____
> _____
>
> When I remember this I: (select one)
> ☐ Need to apologize ☐ Need to forgive ☐ Need to honor that_____
> _____
>
> Initial here: _____ Thank you.

Dear _____, I now need to acknowledge a low point to heal from these painful cords that have bound us in pain for so long. The first low point coming to mind is:_____

When I remember this I: (select one) ☐ Need to apologize ☐ Need to forgive ☐ Need to honor that_____

Initial here: _____ Thank you.

Dear _____, there are only two more high points and two more low points to recall and then I will be free from the pain that binds us. The second high point that comes to mind is: _____

When I remember this I: (select one) ☐ Need to apologize ☐ Need to forgive ☐ Need to honor that_____

The second low point that comes to mind is: _____

When I remember this I: (select one) ☐ Need to apologize ☐ Need to forgive ☐ Need to honor that_____

Initial here: _____ Thank you.

Dear _____, the final high point I need to review is:_____

When I remember this I: (select one) ☐ Need to apologize ☐ Need to forgive ☐ Need to honor that_____

Dear _____, the final low point I need to acknowledge is:_____

When I remember this I: (select one) ☐ Need to apologize ☐ Need to forgive ☐ Need to honor that_____

Initial here: _____ Thank you.

Dear _____, I've learned so much from reviewing our relationship.

In order to be done here once and for all and remove all blocks from receiving, I need to acknowledge that if I had known we were really saying goodbye there is at least one thing I wish I would have done differently and that thing is:_____

Initial _____ Thank you.

And if I had known we were really saying goodbye there is at least one thing I wish I would have done better. That thing is: _____

Initial _____ Thank you.

Finally, _____, I need to acknowledge that in order to heal there is at least one thing I wish I would have done more, and that thing is: _____

Initial _____ Thank you.

Now, _____ the time has come for me to say goodbye, because when something is LEAVING, and the pain attached to this name I write IS leaving, you say goodbye. Not see you later. Goodbye. I will now make my closing statement.
Just because_____,
doesn't mean_____
_____, when I write "GOODBYE" next to your name, the process will be completed. All barriers to receiving caused by the grief of this relationship will also be removed. When you are ready please write "GOODBYE Name" below:

_____

Initial _____ Thank you.

I've noticed in myself that at certain times I'll embellish stories about my childhood because as I'm telling them, I don't feel like they're "strong" enough or compelling enough.

The psychology behind this is way more damaging than a little white lie, so I'm sharing this note in case you catch yourself embellishing too.

ANY TIME YOU LIE FOR ATTENTION ITS A SIGN THAT YOU ARE NOT BEING IN INTEGRITY WITH YOURSELF.

YOU ARE MAKING A PROBLEM WORSE THAT ONLY YOU CAN FIX.

STOP TALKING MID SENTENCE. WALK DOWN A DIFFERENT MENTAL PATH. ITS WORTH IT. I PROMISE.

BE HER NOW

never underestimate how quickly the universe rearranges on your behalf once you have decided.

FUCKLESS: LESSON SIX

What is the fear based story from my past that is blocking me?

In what ways is this keeping me from stepping into my role as a leader?

How do I compare myself to others?

How am I judging myself and my practice?

When I think about this story and how it holds me back, what does it feel like in my body?

Is it an energy that moves fast or slow?

adapted from Spirit Junkie Masterclass

Draw the feeling:

When was the first time you ever felt this way?

READ COMPLETELY THEN ATTEMPT

We're going to use ten breaths to turn up the volume on this feeling from a zero to a ten.

This may or may not be emotional for you, but resolve not to quit.

With each inhale, increase the intensity of feeling.

With each exhale sink into the feeling more..

you should be feeling at a ten on your tenth breath.

When you reach ten, take a deep inhale and exhale loudly through the mouth with your tongue out. Repeat for a total of three.

Observe the lightness of being, locate your pen, and immediately finish the statement on the next page without looking at it now.

RELEASING MY FEAR GIVES ME THE FREEDOM TO:

I have reached the point of no return.

I can no longer lie and abandon myself to make other people feel more comfortable with the fact that I've outgrown pleasing them.

I can no longer do things for approval because when I do, I get further away from who I want to be and I directly stimulate the person I'm trying to leave behind.

If I can't be real with someone, I can't be with someone.
It's not me there anyways.

From this moment forward I will do my absolute best every day to answer honestly, When I'm in a difficult situation where I don't know what to say I'll ask myself "What's the truth? Why do I feel like the truth is not okay here?"

From this moment on I will share truthfully or not share at all. When I am connected to my truth, less words are necessary. When I notice myself explaining excessively, I will ask myself:

Am I in touch with my truth right now?

When faced with difficulty I will ask myself:

Where am I not being truthful with myself about my needs and wants here?

When I'm not sure if I should do something or not I will ask myself:

Am I doing this for the approval?

Let this day mark the beginning of a new life, lived for me.

Signed: Date:

outer self

I admire   for their

I admire   for their

I admire   for their

I admire   for their

I admire   for their

I admire   for their

I admire   for their

what would I do if I were _____?

what would I do if I were _____?

what would I do if I were _____?

what would I do if I were _____ ?

what would I do if I were _____?

what would I do if I were _____ ?

what would I do if I were _____ ?

what would I do if I were _____ ?

what does your warrior say?

what does your magician say?

what does your lover say?

what does your ruler say?

advertising copy:

BUILD ON CUSTOMER AVATAR WORK FROM PILLAR ONE:

WHAT'S THEIR WORST POSSIBLE SCENARIO IF THEY DON'T
SOLVE THEIR BIGGEST PROBLEM?

○ LIST THE SCENARIOS

○ WRITE HOW THE WORST SCENARIO MAKE THEM FEEL

● WRITE WHAT THEIR FAMILY WOULD THINK

○ WRITE WHAT THEIR FRIENDS WOULD THINK

○ WRITE WHAT THEIR BOSS OR CO-WORKERS WOULD
THINK

○ WRITE WHAT WOULD HAPPEN TO THEIR CAREER OR
PERSONAL LIFESTYLE

○ WRITE WHAT WOULD HAPPEN TO THEM FINANCIALLY

○ WRITE WHAT WOULD HAPPEN TO THEM PROFESSIONALLY

● WRITE WHAT WOULD HAPPEN TO THEM PERSONALLY

○ WRITE WHAT YOU THINK THEY ARE SECRETLY AFRAID OF

BUILD ON CUSTOMER AVATAR WORK FROM PILLAR ONE:

WHAT IS THE BEST CASE SCENARIO IF THEY ARE ABLE TO
SOLVE THEIR BIGGEST PROBLEM?

● WRITE WHAT THE PERFECT SOLUTIONS WOULD LOOK LIKE

● WRITE WHAT YOU THINK THEY REALLY WANT MORE THAN
ANYTHING

● WRITE WHAT YOU THINK THEY WOULD BE WILLING TO PAY
ALMOST ANYTHING FOR

● WRITE HOW YOUR PRODUCT OR SERVICE CAN MEET THEIR
NEEDS AND DESIRES

● WRITE HOW YOUR BUSINESS CAN HELP THEM SOLVE
THEIR PROBLEMS

● WRITE WHAT YOU ARE REALLY TRYING TO PROVIDE THEM
WITH YOUR OFFER

191

CREATE A SHORT STORY ABOUT YOUR IDEAL PROSPECT BASED ONTHE WORK WE DID HERE AND IN CUSTOMER AVATAR.

● INCLUDE DETAILS ABOUT THEIR LIFE AND PROFESSIONAL BACKGROUND

● EXPLAIN THE IMPACT THEIR PROBLEM IS HAVING

● DISCUSS WHAT THIS PROBLEM IS MAKING THEM FEEL

● DISCUSS WHAT KEEPS THEM UP AT NIGHT

● DESCRIBE WHAT FRUSTRATIONS THAT KEEP COMING UP FOR THEM

● DISCUSS WHAT THEY NEED MORE THAN ANYTHING

● DESCRIBE HOW YOUR BUSINESS CAN PROVIDE A SOLUTION FOR THEM

WRITE AS MUCH AS YOU CAN

developing a kink

FUCKLESS: LESSON EIGHT

WORRY ENDS WHEN YOU TELL THE TRUTH.

ONAMI

RANDOM TRUTHS THAT MAKE IT EASIER TO SAY GOODBYE TO PEOPLE

if someone wants to change you so bad maybe they should find a friend they like as is so they don't have to worry so much.

the customers that leave when you're real are the ones who were never going to pay you

by being open about what you believe and who you are, you make it easy for your niche to find you.

anyone who suggests their happiness and comfort should be considered over yours serves no purpose in your life whatsoever.

EVOLVE OR REPEAT?

not everyone will like it.

do it anyways.

not everyone can handle success.

two thirds of Destiny's Child did not go on to be Beyonce.

I said it.

vetting the paying customers from the non paying customers, and the real friends from the fake friends is as simple as choosing to tell the truth about exactly how you feel in the moment instead of faking it because you assume they can't handle you.

it's your time.

nothing can stop an idea whose time has come.

there is a place in you without fear
there is a place in you without anxiety
there is a place in you without
thoughts
there is a place in you without effort
you can relax in this place
this place is I AM
and here
being is enough

O N A M I

new level
new devil

Point Eight, Presentation, is as far as I can take you in a book by spiritual law. What you do with this is up to you, and also up to how it's received.

It can be very hard to get that first bit of feedback from someone you weren't expecting to outgrow so fast. It can be very hard to hear someone close to you say something like "I'm worried about your mental health" .

They have every right to think this, honestly. They had no idea you were faking it this whole time up until now. This "new" you is completely unlike anyone they've ever met before and this is especially hard if they're observing you from a distance.

They also HAVE to give you some resistance cause you've done all this spiritual work to expedite the journey to living as your real self, so by spiritual law they have to show up and invite you to repeat the pattern at which point I hope you'll remember yourself and your aim and maybe utilize some of the many flashing neon signs I've included across the pages. These have ALL been taped to my walls.

It's a test.
Life is school.
Re-cognize the gift, and keep going.

At the point where someone challenges you, it could be really easy to give up. But you look back on all the work we've done here in this space and get renewed energy. You think about your core gifts, the truth of who you really are. You think about the Painkillers worksheets we've done here and how every relationship does have it's ups and downs, and maybe you can see on the horizon the next level of truth this interaction is nudging you towards. Maybe when you review this relationship (we'll throw an extra worksheet in for you on the next page) you realize that it is a little more complicated than you remember, or maybe simpler in the sense that the behavior causing the issue has not changed over time.

Sure, maybe you're guilty of everything they accuse you of, but haven't we been through this? Is it really something so original, or is it just an echo of the criticisms you usually hurl at yourself? And even so, you've never claimed to be perfect. If someone is spending their time thinking about how you should live your life on their terms and if you don't they'll verbally abuse you and call you names that make it seem like saying no to this person you usually say yes to indicates psychological instability on your end - that's a THEM problem.

Don't make a you problem out of a them problem.

Until then, submit as many questions as you want in the Fuckless Q and A forum on Safehouse, and I will see you for the next video where we answer all of them!

it's going to take you some practice but now that you've committed to it, it will only get easier. Every day will uncover a new and beautiful truth. Every time you feel the weight of that personality coming on, making you insecure, you'll be able to check yourself. You can ask "Am I doing this for approval?"and see if there isn't a part of you that's insisting only a false version of you could possibly manage the task at hand. This is just ridiculous. You can relax the personality.

If you find yourself wrangling with social anxiety, I recommend taking the time to think of a question you could always enjoy hearing the answer to. For me it's "what's the most unexplainable thing you've ever seen?".

By having a question that always opens up a cool story at the ready, if you ever find yourself in an anxious situation, just ask them your question and watch how the pressure to converse is taken off you completely.

I want to thank you for choosing yourself in this way with me as your guide. I couldn't think of a greater gift than being able to "take your heavy coat" for you so you can dance.

Of all the beautiful flowers in this garden, I think you are the most beautiful. Welcome to your bloom.

brand strategy worksheet:

WHO ARE YOU?

WHY DO YOU DO WHAT YOU DO?

WHAT DO YOU WANT TO ACHIEVE?

HOW ARE YOU GOING TO DO IT?

WHO DO YOU SERVE?

WHAT IS YOUR NICHE?

WHAT DO YOU BELIEVE?

HOW DO YOU PRESENT YOURSELF?

HOW DO YOU COMMUNICATE?

WHAT DO YOU WANT TO COMMUNICATE?

Painkiller (one sheet)
an ONAMI initiative

Date: _____ Name: _____

Step One: The Emotional Truth

DISCLAIMER: This worksheet is yours and trust me, you don't want anyone else to read it. This worksheet contains the emotional truth. You don't need to fact-check yourself, be exact, or even make sense. This may or may not be emotional for you.

Are you willing to tell the emotional truth here, even if you're the only one who sees the story this way?

☐ Willing ☐ Open ☐ Unsure ☐ Unwilling

Step Two: Diagnosing Grief

Conflicting feelings occur when a great change results in unfinished business. Some examples of a great change would be: loss of a job, moving, breaking up with someone, a change in routine, or the birth of a child.

Have you recently experienced a great change?
☐ Yes ☐ No ☐ Not Sure

> Unfinished business is things you wish you did **differently, better, or more.** Do you feel like you have unfinished business with something or someone?
> ☐ Yes ☐ No ☐ Not Sure

Unfinished business creates painful energetic cords that make it hard for us to "forgive & forget". Unfinished business may feel like reaching for something or someone that was always there only to find out that when you need it one last time, it's still not there. Unfinished business may also feel like, reaching for something or someone who was never there, only to find out when you need it one last time, it's still not there.

> Are you having a hard time forgiving and forgetting something or someone who was **always** there?
> ☐ Yes ☐ No ☐ Not Sure

> Are you having a hard time forgiving and forgetting something or someone who was **never** there?
> ☐ Yes ☐ No ☐ Not Sure

Step Three: Completion Letter

In writing the completion letter, you will be closing the unfinished business causing you optional pain. You are not saying goodbye to the person, place, or thing. There is no need to contact the person, living, dead, or unborn for healing to occur. There is no need to tell anyone you've forgiven them. You will be saying goodbye to the pain.

> Are you ready to begin? ☐ Yes ☐ No ☐ Not Sure
> Initial here: _____ Thank you.

> Please write the name of the person, place or thing you are grieving.
>
> Dear _____, I've been reviewing our relationship and there are some things I need to say.
>
> My first memory with you is: _____
> _____
>
> When I revisit this memory, I must acknowledge that:_____
> _____
>
> Initial here: _____ Thank you.

> Dear _____ as I continue this journey towards completing our story, I need to acknowledge that in all relationships there are ups and downs. I need to acknowledge that in our relationship, there were ups and downs. In order to heal, I need to honor these stories with no criticism, analysis, or judgment. This may or may not be emotional. But I will not skip any.
> Initial _____ Thank you.
>
> _____, the first high point in our relationship that comes to mind is:_____
> _____
>
> When I remember this I: (select one)
> ☐ Need to apologize ☐ Need to forgive ☐ Need to honor that_____
> _____
>
> Initial here: _____ Thank you.

Dear _____, I now need to acknowledge a low point to heal from these painful cords that have bound us in pain for so long. The first low point coming to mind is:_____

When I remember this I: (select one) ☐ Need to apologize ☐ Need to forgive ☐ Need to honor that_____

Initial here: _____ Thank you.

Dear _____, there are only two more high points and two more low points to recall and then I will be free from the pain that binds us. The second high point that comes to mind is: _____

When I remember this I: (select one) ☐ Need to apologize ☐ Need to forgive ☐ Need to honor that_____

The second low point that comes to mind is: _____

When I remember this I: (select one) ☐ Need to apologize ☐ Need to forgive ☐ Need to honor that_____

Initial here: _____ Thank you.

Dear _____, the final high point I need to review is:_____

When I remember this I: (select one) ☐ Need to apologize ☐ Need to forgive ☐ Need to honor that_____

Dear _____, the final low point I need to acknowledge is:_____

When I remember this I: (select one) ☐ Need to apologize ☐ Need to forgive ☐ Need to honor that_____

Initial here: _____ Thank you.

Dear _____, I've learned so much from reviewing our relationship.

In order to be done here once and for all and remove all blocks from receiving, I need to acknowledge that if I had known we were really saying goodbye there is at least one thing I wish I would have done differently and that thing is:_____

Initial _____ Thank you.

And if I had known we were really saying goodbye there is at least one thing I wish I would have done better.
That thing is: _____

Initial _____ Thank you.

Finally, _____, I need to acknowledge that in order to heal there is at least one thing I wish I would have done more, and that thing is: _____

Initial _____ Thank you.

Now, _____ the time has come for me to say goodbye, because when something is LEAVING, and the pain attached to this name I write IS leaving, you say goodbye. Not see you later. Goodbye. I will now make my closing statement.
Just because_____,

doesn't mean_____
_____, when I write "GOODBYE" next to your name, the process will be completed. All barriers to receiving caused by the grief of this relationship will also be removed. When you are ready please write "GOODBYE Name" below:

_____

Initial _____ Thank you.

Painkiller (one sheet)

an ONAMI initiative

Date: _____ Name: _____

Step One: The Emotional Truth

DISCLAIMER: This worksheet is yours and trust me, you don't want anyone else to read it. This worksheet contains the emotional truth. You don't need to fact-check yourself, be exact, or even make sense. This may or may not be emotional for you.

Are you willing to tell the emotional truth here, even if you're the only one who sees the story this way?

☐ Willing ☐ Open ☐ Unsure ☐ Unwilling

Step Two: Diagnosing Grief

Conflicting feelings occur when a great change results in unfinished business. Some examples of a great change would be: loss of a job, moving, breaking up with someone, a change in routine, or the birth of a child.

Have you recently experienced a great change?
☐ Yes ☐ No ☐ Not Sure

> Unfinished business is things you wish you did **differently, better, or more.** Do you feel like you have unfinished business with something or someone?
> ☐ Yes ☐ No ☐ Not Sure

Unfinished business creates painful energetic cords that make it hard for us to "forgive & forget". Unfinished business may feel like reaching for something or someone that was always there only to find out that when you need it one last time, it's still not there. Unfinished business may also feel like, reaching for something or someone who was never there, only to find out when you need it one last time, it's still not there.

> Are you having a hard time forgiving and forgetting something or someone who was **always** there?
> ☐ Yes ☐ No ☐ Not Sure

> Are you having a hard time forgiving and forgetting something or someone who was **never** there?
> ☐ Yes ☐ No ☐ Not Sure

Step Three: Completion Letter

In writing the completion letter, you will be closing the unfinished business causing you optional pain. You are not saying goodbye to the person, place, or thing, only the pain. There is no need to contact the person, living, dead, or unborn for healing to occur. There is no need to tell anyone you've forgiven them. You will be saying goodbye to the pain.

> Are you ready to begin? ☐ Yes ☐ No ☐ Not Sure
> Initial here: _____ Thank you.

> Please write the name of the person, place or thing you are grieving.
>
> Dear _____, I've been reviewing our relationship and there are some things I need to say.
>
> My first memory with you is: _____
> _____
>
> When I revisit this memory, I must acknowledge that:_____
> _____
>
> Initial here: _____ Thank you.

> Dear _____ as I continue this journey towards completing our story, I need to acknowledge that in all relationships there are ups and downs. I need to acknowledge that in our relationship, there were ups and downs. In order to heal, I need to honor these stories with no criticism, analysis, or judgment. This may or may not be emotional. But I will not skip any.
> Initial _____ Thank you.
> _____, the first high point in our relationship that comes to mind is:_____
> _____
>
> When I remember this I: (select one)
> ☐ Need to apologize ☐ Need to forgive ☐ Need to honor that_____
> _____
>
> Initial here: _____ Thank you.

Dear _____, I now need to acknowledge a low point to heal from these painful cords that have bound us in pain for so long. The first low point coming to mind is:_____

_____

When I remember this I: (select one) ☐ Need to apologize ☐ Need to forgive ☐ Need to honor that_____

_____

Initial here: _____ Thank you.

Dear _____, there are only two more high points and two more low points to recall and then I will be free from the pain that binds us. The second high point that comes to mind is: _____

_____

When I remember this I: (select one) ☐ Need to apologize ☐ Need to forgive ☐ Need to honor that_____

_____

The second low point that comes to mind is: _____

_____

When I remember this I: (select one) ☐ Need to apologize ☐ Need to forgive ☐ Need to honor that_____

_____

Initial here: _____ Thank you.

Dear _____, the final high point I need to review is:_____

_____

When I remember this I: (select one) ☐ Need to apologize ☐ Need to forgive ☐ Need to honor that_____

_____

Dear _____, the final low point I need to acknowledge is:_____

_____

When I remember this I: (select one) ☐ Need to apologize ☐ Need to forgive ☐ Need to honor that_____

_____

Initial here: _____ Thank you.

Dear _____, I've learned so much from reviewing our relationship.

In order to be done here once and for all and remove all blocks from receiving, I need to acknowledge that if I had known we were really saying goodbye there is at least one thing I wish I would have done differently and that thing is:_____

_____

Initial _____ Thank you.

And if I had known we were really saying goodbye there is at least one thing I wish I would have done better.
That thing is: _____

Initial _____ Thank you.

Finally, _____, I need to acknowledge that in order to heal there is at least one thing I wish I would have done more, and that thing is:_____

Initial _____ Thank you.

Now, _____ the time has come for me to say goodbye, because when something is LEAVING, and the pain attached to this name I write IS leaving, you say goodbye. Not see you later. Goodbye. I will now make my closing statement.
Just because_____,

doesn't mean_____
_____, when I write "GOODBYE" next to your name, the process will be completed. All barriers to receiving caused by the grief of this relationship will also be removed. When you are ready please write "GOODBYE Name" below:

_____

Initial _____ Thank you.

notes

Made in the USA
Monee, IL
10 October 2023

44346309R00122